# THE ART OF THE BOOK HUSTLE: No Shame, Just Gain

by Keidi Obi Awadu
for the Conscious Rasta Press
Copyright 2023

Black Star Media
9515 Cherrydale Ct.,
Las Vegas NV 89147 U.S.A.
All rights reserved under
U.S. copyright law

Please email me (Keidi@chefkeidi.com) to schedule an interview, workshop, personal consultation, or other interaction on this wonderful new way of living, working, and sustainability. The number to my office is 323.902.2919 Pacific Time, from 1-6 PM.

Keywords: writing, publishing, memoir, history, science, self-help, creative arts, authors, fiction, nonfiction, books, future studies, business, marketing, publicity, poetry, education, copyright, research, coaching, leadership, wisdom, promotion, never-give-up

"All good books are alike in that they are truer than if they had really happened and after you are finished reading one you will feel that all that happened to you and afterwards it all belongs to you: the good and the bad, the ecstasy, the remorse and sorrow, the people and the places and how the weather was. If you can get it so that you can give that to people, then you are a writer."
— *Ernest Hemingway*

"If you have any young friends who aspire to become writers, the second greatest favor you can do them is to present them with copies of The Elements of Style. The first greatest, of course, is to shoot them now, while they're happy." — *Dorothy Purker*

"If you have a dream, don't just sit there. Gather courage to believe that you can succeed and leave no stone unturned to make it a reality." — *Dr. Roopleen*

"It is literally true that you can succeed best and quickest by helping others to succeed." — *Napolean Hill*

# Contents

Introduction ................................................................1

   Pimps and Hustlers ...............................................1

   Inform, Inspire, and Excite Positive Change .................3

What's In a Name? ....................................................7

   Living and Loving the Writer's Craft .........................7

   Why Obsess Over Book Titles? .................................8

The Hustler's Motivation ..........................................10

   Hustlers Be Like Sharks ........................................10

Preparing to Succeed ...............................................14

   Think of Your Plan as a Treasure Map ....................14

   I Sure Wish I Had Said That....................................15

Time to Get Your Hustle On........................................19

   Suffering for the Errors of My Youth .......................19

   Get Started with Your Hustler's Strategic Action Plan ..........20

Important Components of a Book to Consider .............24

   Front Matter .........................................................24

   Body Text .............................................................27

   Back Matter..........................................................27

Proven Strategies to Increase Sales.............................32

   If It Were Easy, Then Everyone Would Do It, Right? .............32

   Building an author platform ...................................33

   Engaging with the target audience...........................33

   The Power of Emotional Appeal in Marketing .........33

   The Logic of Effective Marketing: Appeal to Reason.............35

   The Art of Scarcity: Drive Demand Through Exclusivity ........37

Leveraging book reviews and endorsements.................38

Utilizing effective book covers and blurbs ..............38

Employing targeted online advertising....................38

Utilizing book promotion sites and newsletters..........39

Offering promotions and discounts.......................39

Participating in book signings and events ..............39

Collaborating with other authors .......................39

Continuously improving writing and editing .............40

Teaching Online Courses.................................40

Create a Landing Page for Your Book Funnel .............42

Great Insights from Kindlepreneur.......................44

Print-on-Demand: The Book Hustler's New Tool ..........44

Insights on Building Book Sales from Kindlepreneur ....46

Amazon Kindle Rankings.................................47

Trigger Words for Books ...............................49

Best Book Promo Websites ..............................51

Kindlepreneur's Book Launch Strategy..................53

Kindle Keyword Strategy for Nonfiction Authors ........55

Marketing Strategies Checklist ........................58

You Are Ready to Market Your Books ....................96

Bibliography & Resources ..............................98

Index..................................................99

# Introduction

*"Don't let mental blocks control you.*
*Set yourself free. Confront your fear and turn the*
*mental blocks into building blocks."*

*"The world's greatest achievers have been those*
*who have always stayed focused on their goals*
*and have been consistent in their efforts."*
— Dr. Roopleen, Words to inspire the winner in YOU

## Pimps and Hustlers

When we think about the common comprehension of a hustler, the image of a pimp might come to mind. This narrow perception is because the culture within which we live celebrates these low-down characterizations; a pimp is someone that we love to hate. Sometimes, the image of a hustler is someone who games the system, often cheating, to gain something valuable far lower than a fair exchange.

Common synonyms for "hustler" include prostitute, crook, shark, swindler, cheater, grifter, fast-talker, rip-off artist, or scammer. Such individuals are considered dishonest, corrupt, untrustworthy, unscrupulous, and deceitful.

Yet, depending on our experience and orientation, being regarded as a hustler can have many positive associations. A hustler can possess and project multiple desirable attributes. Among these, I would include observant, quick-minded, quick to grasp at opportunity, multi-talented, an over-the-horizon perspective, determined to succeed, relentless, resilient, and self-motivated.

In *The Art of the Book Hustle*, I want to clarify our projection of the hustler and their mission to sell literature in the most positive light possible. I want to portray the hustler foremost as an artist who is creative, visionary, bold, relentless, and genuinely interested in the well-being and best outcome to those who consume the product, which, in my case, is transformative literature and communications.

I will demonstrate the careful attention that goes into crafting books and the duty to the larger society that many authors demonstrate. I have written a lot of books and too often feel that they are underappreciated. This reflects hard on the soul of the literary artist. In modern society, the call for higher learning and literacy is often overridden by the ease of social media triflings and the seduction of streaming videos.

From my perspective, an ideal society prioritizes literacy, scientific examination, comprehension of complex ideas, and competence in problem-solving; thus, I write.

Beyond writing, I am determined to expand my skills into better marketing and distribution of the products that I have crafted. I've determined that I've benefited greatly from a lifetime of exposure to the information that has passed before me over the decades of experiences that I have had in the world. Therefore, I'm determined to share these experiences and my written recollections with all seeking enlightenment from my ongoing legacy.

## Inform, Inspire, and Excite Positive Change

Maybe I am a dreamer; perhaps I am holding onto values that are struggling to remain central in this modern, high-tech, and materialistic society. Yet, I still believe in the higher aspirations of humanity. The hustler in me wants to do good for myself and my family, yet not tolerate injury to the larger society during self-advancement. Past generations have clearly demonstrated this spirit of "the greatest good" for all members of the larger community and society. We can build upon these high values that served as the foundation of generational morality, logic, and sustainable progress.

I was raised in an environment that held high value in functional literacy. My family was scientific, highly literate, competent across various specialties, and respectful of education and order in the learning environment. Within such a value system, one finds reward at all levels during the period of life when our education is central to maturation. Just as my parents created this value system for their children, I was able to foster a similar cultural environment with my daughters' mother. Within this zeitgeist, they thrived and are now in the early stages of orienting the next generation.

For the majority of us, our parents, grandparents, and ancestors were disciplined, bold, and determined. They were able to calculate the long-term benefits of short-term sacrifice. They always considered how the elders and the wise ones would judge their behaviors, even when they were outside of view or scrutinized by those who would pass judgment. The culture of that time taught us all to self-regulate our behaviors and to preserve our dignity through our actions. From my perspective as a member of the Baby Boomer generation, I would say that our parents and grandparents did a great job passing on these values that contribute to the continuity of life's most cherished traditions.

May my words, meditations, and articulations assist you to rise to your highest potential. I do my best to represent this intergenerational tradition of excellence in all areas of humanity. When I put these traditions into books coherently and inspiringly, I feel that I am doing my part for this generation to preserve all that is good. But, beyond creating a conserving narrative, I know these ideas will mean little or nothing if they remain confined to the smallest audiences. Therefore, I must hustle to get my most transformative conceptualizations to the widest audiences possible.

As members of a group, we have obligations to engage in specific duties that provide long-term benefits to the collective; the group must survive by every means. As one looks closely at analytical data to gauge how well the community is doing, there is room to be cautious and concerned. My books have largely been built upon examining life patterns challenged by widespread inadequacy and failure. I write about health, education, media, societal values, political affairs, corporate machinations, leadership inadequacies, sustainability, and other affairs impacting the commons. We're not doing so well along this frontier, and I have determined that much of what we now have access to is unsustainable unless we can foster major corrective changes – a **Paradigm Shift**.

Our children and future generations must be primary beneficiaries of the commitments that we make in our lifetime. But we've got to do better. Through the methodologies shared in this book, independent writers and publishers can advance how our literary artistry is distributed. The more people synchronize their empowering intentions, the more we can measure progress for the individuals and the group. Thus, **The Art of the Book Hustle** is another way to advance humanity, culture, and progress for the greatest proportion of the population. It is well intended.

With this book, I seek to inform, inspire, and excite greater opportunities for us all to rise to the heights of sustainable accomplishment.  In this book, I write much about the Hustler's motivation.  I'll close this introduction with this inspiring prose from **Shannon L. Alder**, an inspirational author, and therapist who has been quoted in over 100 books by relationship authors and in online magazine articles:

> "I write to find strength.
> I write to become the person that hides inside me.
> I write to light the way through the darkness for others.
> I write to be seen and heard.
> I write to be near those I love.
> I write by accident, promptings, purposefully and anywhere there is paper.
> I write because my heart speaks a different language that someone needs to hear.
> I write past the embarrassment of exposure.
> I write because hypocrisy doesn't need answers, rather it needs questions to heal.
> I write myself out of nightmares.
> I write because I am nostalgic, romantic and demand happy endings.
> I write to remember.
> I write knowing conversations don't always take place.
> I write because speaking can't be reread.
> I write to sooth a mind that races.

I write because you can play on the page like a child left alone in the sand.

I write because my emotions belong to the moon; high tide, low tide.

I write knowing I will fall on my words, but no one will say it was for very long.

I write because I want to paint the world the way I see love should be.

I write to provide a legacy.

I write to make sense out of senselessness.

I write knowing I will be killed by my own words, stabbed by critics, crucified by both misunderstanding and understanding.

I write for the haters, the lovers, the lonely, the brokenhearted and the dreamers.

I write because one day someone will tell me that my emotions were not a waste of time.

I write because God loves stories.

I write because one day I will be gone, but what I believed and felt will live on."[1]

---

[1] Shannon L. Alder Sayings and Quotes, cited on the online site of Wise Sayings.

# What's In a Name?

*"Have a bias towards action – let's see something happen now. You can break that big plan into small steps and take the first step right away."*
– Indira Gandhi

## Living and Loving the Writer's Craft

I love the craft of writing and publishing. I have pursued this for about forty years since I got my first published reviews in a Columbus, Ohio, entertainment publication. It was quite a memory when I saw my first reviews of albums from Bill Withers, The Emotions, Minnie Riperton, and other favorite musical artists. A bonus was that I got a chance to access their newest albums before they were released to the public and attend concerts at no cost.

Fast forward from the 1970s to the 1990s, I'd spent two decades relocating from Columbus to Atlanta, briefly in Seattle, and finally settling into metropolitan Los Angeles. There, I started writing again, this time focusing on cultural issues and ethnic empowerment. My friend Warren Daniels created a community-centered newspaper for which he welcomed my regular contributions, the *Carson Community News*. It renewed the thrill of seeing my byline in each publication and provoked my curiosity to know more about the key issues that would engage an audience.

Over those years, I was published in several magazines and newspapers and contributed to book anthologies. In the early

1990s, I started focusing on more engaging research, eventually graduating to writing a series of nonfiction books.

With book writing, one's focus must become more long-term. In theory, a book title must be more durable than music and concert reviews or commentary around local political, cultural, or artistic events. From my standpoint, writing and publishing books is akin to documenting history in a way expected to transfer from generation to generation. It is an awesome responsibility when you think about it. As a book writer, I can create a permanent legacy – that is IF what I've written can hold the public interest over time.

I love the craft and am quite proud of what I have contributed to the collected wisdom of society, my generation, and my relevant skill sets. Of the myriad of tactical steps to getting my books written and published, one of the most critical tasks is what to name the book. This takes more effort than many people may imagine and can make or break a book's reception to an audience.

## Why Obsess Over Book Titles?

A title can convey so many different conceptual frameworks. It can be funny or ominous, high-minded or low-browed. A book title can attract or dispel a particularly concerned audience. I have come up with some really good titles over the years that I thought would quickly grab readers' attention. Some of them bombed, and some of them hit. As my publishing experience persists, I find that getting a title right is so absolutely important.

So, for this book on the subject of self-marketing your independently-published book, selecting a catchy title became an engaging task. I intended to make this book fun and not an overburdening job. Here is a list of ideas that paraded through my head:

- Sell More Books Than Your Crazy Aunt Agatha
- The Art of Book Hustling
- No Shame, No Gain
- Searching for the Perfect Book Title
- Unleash the Book Sales Beast Within
- Sell More Books Than Your Cat Has Lives
- The Naked Truth About Selling Books
- The Book Sales Bible: Thou Shalt Sell More Books.
- Selling More Books and Still Having Fun

As you can judge by now, the idea of "The Art of Book Hustling" caught my fancy. It reminded me of the world-famous book, **The Art of War**. The idea of the Hustle reminded me of one of my favorite funny movies, the Chinese-made *Kung Fu Hustle*.

This stuck with me, and I hope it sticks with many people, especially independent writers and publishers. Now we've gotten past the title, let's focus our attention on compelling content to make the book a great and productive investment.

Let's get this hustle started. There is a whole new world begging to be created. There are many rivers to cross and mountains to climb on our magnificent journey to a marvelous destination.

We've got a lot of books to sell.

# The Hustler's Motivation

*"I am like the shark that must keep swimming, or else it might suffocate."* – Keidi Awadu

## Hustlers Be Like Sharks

The quote that I used to introduce this chapter is based on a biological imperative that is well-known within the marine world.

> "Obligate ram ventilators" are sharks that have lost the ability, and the necessary anatomy, for buccal pumping, and instead can only respire using ram ventilation. Sharks from this group (which includes great white, mako and whale sharks) would indeed die from lack of oxygen if they stopped swimming.[2]

A strong inner drive wants you to bust through any barriers to blockbuster book sales; that sounds like "ram ventilation" to me. That driving factor is what we commonly know as the *Hustler's Motivation*. It's time to let that beast come out to play. Many people are consistent, creative, and respected hustlers in life. What characteristics of such go-getters have been written about?

Let's examine the characteristics that can be considered as representing the *Hustler's Motivation*.

1.   **Open-Minded** – Think outside the box; if it is already being done, especially by multiple competitors, then you are

---

[2] Must Sharks Keep Swimming to Stay Alive? by Joseph Castro, Live Science, May 29, 2013

obligated to break the mold by doing it uniquely, thereby distinguish yourself from the masses.

2. **Consciously Aware** – Always being observant of details within the environment that one inhabits is a prime characteristic of the Hustler's Motivation. This is particularly important regarding the marketplace.

3. **Seizes All Opportunities** – Take your creative impulses seriously. Develop the habit of constant notetaking. Don't let a brilliant insight disappear because you didn't take a moment to jot down your thoughts. Many brilliant ideas have awakened me in the middle of the night, yet often, those ideas disappear with the next round of REM sleep.

4. **Passionate**: Hustlers are driven by a deep passion for their work. They pursue endeavors that align with their interests, values, and talents, allowing their passion to fuel their motivation and determination.

5. **Ambitious**: Hustlers possess a strong desire to achieve and succeed. They set ambitious goals for themselves and are willing to put in the necessary effort and dedication to make them a reality.

6. **Persistent**: Hustlers understand that success rarely comes overnight. They are resilient despite challenges and setbacks, persistently working towards their goals despite resistance.

7. **Self-Motivated**: Hustlers are self-starters who possess an internal drive to excel. They don't rely solely on external validation or motivation; instead, they have an innate ability to push themselves forward and stay focused on their objectives. Hustlers are masters of self-determination.

8. **Growth Mindset**: Hustlers embrace a growth mindset, believing their abilities and skills can be developed through

dedication and hard work. They view failures as opportunities for learning and constantly seek ways to improve themselves.

9. **Adaptability**: Hustlers are adaptable and flexible in their approach. They understand the importance of adjusting their strategies, embracing change, and being open to new ideas to stay ahead in dynamic environments.

10. **Creativity**: Hustlers often think outside the box and develop innovative solutions to problems. They are willing to take risks, explore unconventional approaches, and challenge the status quo to find new opportunities for success.

11. **Disciplined and Focused**: Hustlers exhibit discipline in managing their time, setting priorities, and staying focused on their goals. They are skilled at organizing their efforts and avoiding distractions to maintain productivity and progress.

12. **Resilient**: Hustlers have strong mental and emotional resilience. They bounce back from failures, rejection, or criticism, using these experiences as steppingstones for growth and self-improvement.

13. **Networkers and Relationship-Builders**: Hustlers understand the value of building relationships and networks. They actively seek out connections with like-minded individuals, mentors, industry experts, and potential collaborators to expand their opportunities and gain support.

14. **Continuous Learning**: Hustlers have a thirst for knowledge and are lifelong learners. They invest in personal and professional development, seeking educational resources, attending workshops, and staying updated on industry trends.

15. **Integrity and Authenticity**: Hustlers value honesty, integrity, and authenticity in their actions and interactions. Their genuine approach builds trust and credibility, ensuring their work and relationships are built on solid foundations.

16. **Financial Independence and Freedom**: Hustlers often strive for economic autonomy and freedom to live on their own terms. They are motivated by the desire to create opportunities for themselves, take control of their financial well-being, and live life on their own terms.

17. **Purposeful and Impactful**: Hustlers seek meaning and purpose in their work. They are driven by the desire to make a positive impact, whether on a small scale or a larger societal level, and contribute to the greater good.

18. **Personal Fulfillment**: Ultimately, hustlers are motivated by a deep sense of personal fulfillment. They find joy and satisfaction in pursuing their passions, achieving their goals, and seeing the results of their hard work.

19. **Love the Art of the Deal**: Some people love to wheel and deal, which is a notable trait among those with the *Hustler's Motivation*. They know they can be very convincing as they are also quite astute at examining the many details of an ideal opportunity.

20. **Get in early, and get in deep!** – Hustlers want to 1) get in, 2) get in early, and 3) get in deep to seize the moment and advance their long-term position.

Not all hustlers possess every characteristic on this list, and motivations can vary from individual to individual. However, these are common traits and motivations often associated with those who consistently strive for success and make a positive impact through their efforts.

# Preparing to Succeed

*"Before anything else, preparation is the key to success."* – Alexander Graham Bell

## Think of Your Plan as a Treasure Map

We have heard and tried our best to fully comprehend every affirmation, cliché, and warning about planning to succeed. We know this to be true when Tariq Siddique wrote: "If you are failing to plan, you are planning to fail."

So we seek to find and activate every motivator that can be brought to our advantage at the commencement of every transforming journey. Such is the moment, the crossroads where I, the teacher, and you, the student, find ourselves today. When I write a book on life-enhancement and skills development, I write as much, or more for my benefit, along with those I expect to be the most valuable students.

At our best, we are both teachers and students throughout the entire course of life. As much as I intend to inform, inspire, and excite you to succeed as an author, publisher, or book marketer, I wish similar abundance for myself. This is the true and revealed purpose for committing to publishing The Art of the Book Hustle.

So, before we do the work, let's hear a few motivating insights from those whose accomplishments have placed their names into the historical record. One day, you and I also wish to be remembered for our great works and the inspiration others took from our experiences.

## I Sure Wish I Had Said That

During times when I feel I need to psych myself up to the great task before me, I use the Internet and my favorite search engine to look up quotes on any topic. Here's what I found with the inquiry, "list of quotes to inspire success."

1. "The trouble with many plans is that they are based on the way things are now. To be successful, your personal plan must focus on what you want, not what you have." – Nido Qubein – **Nido Qubein** is a Lebanese American motivational speaker and businessman, current president of High Point University. His is a common and key message about thinking, acting, and future planning, wisely anticipating what developing factors will affect our ability to accomplish our goals.

2. "Unless commitment is made, there are only promises and hopes; but no plans." – Peter F. Drucker – **Peter F. Drucker** was an Austrian-American management consultant and author whose writings contributed to modern management theory. I take these words to heart. Too often, I have caught myself talking about planning and changes for the future, yet not seen sufficient committed actions to actualize the visions. "Hope" is not a sound business strategic pathway.

3. "As for the future, your task is not to foresee it, but to enable it." – Antoine de Saint Exupery – Born **Antoine Marie Jean-Baptiste Roger** at the beginning of the 20th Century, was a French writer and poet. De Saint Exupery's words remind me that being a futurist is insufficient if I lack preparation to be an activist and change-agent. This quote closely mirrors one I've often shared, "The future belongs to those best prepared to create that future today."

4. "Before anything else, preparation is the key to success." –
Alexander Graham Bell – This Scottish-born inventor
**Alexander Graham Bell** was a scientist and engineer credited
with patenting the first practical telephone. He also co-
founded the American Telephone and Telegraph Company.
Again, we are admonished to consider the immense value of
preparation as a prerequisite to achieving great goals in life.
It has often been said that success is 90% preparation and
10% luck.

5. "Plan for what is difficult while it is easy, do what is great
while it is still small." – Sun Tzu – The legendary Chinese
philosopher **Sun Tzu** was a military strategist and general,
considered one of the wisest sages in world history.  His
words remind us that anticipating the tough work ahead
should inspire one to accomplish the easy tasks with creative
precision so that when things get more difficult, our
momentum will not leave us short.

6. "When something is important enough, you do it even if the
odds are not in your favor." – Elon Musk – **Elon R. Musk** has
an impressive resume as a business magnate and investor.
Musk is the founder, chairman, CEO and chief technology
officer of SpaceX, Tesla, Inc., and now the owner and CTO of
Twitter, a co-founder of Neuralink and OpenAI, and more.
His inspiring words combine with his impressive record to
encourage us to risk the odds when our passion is deeply
committed to noble and worthy goals.  This quote reminds
me of the Nike motto: *Just Do It!*

7. "Have a bias towards action – let's see something happen
now. You can break that big plan into small steps and take
the first step right away." – Indira Gandhi – **Indira
Priyadarshini Gandhi**, née Nehru, was an Indian politician

who became India's first female prime minister, serving three consecutive terms from 1966–77, and a fourth term from 1980. She was assassinated in 1984. Her words ring reminiscent of the cliché "a journey of a thousand miles begins with one step," to which I add that such journey is *not* merely making that first but continuing to step, step, step in a steady rhythm – eventually you will reach your destination.

8. "Someone's sitting in the shade today because someone planted a tree a long time ago." – Warren Buffett – **Warren E. Buffett**, the American business magnate, is an investor, and philanthropist. The chairman and CEO of Berkshire Hathaway, he is one of the best-known foundational investors worldwide, and as of 2023, has a net worth estimated to be $117 billion. His proverb is reminiscent of a similar Chinese proverb/riddle: "When is the best time to plant a fruit tree? Twenty years ago. When is the second-best time to plant a fruit tree? Today!"

9. "Planning is bringing the future into the present so that you can do something about it now." – Alan Lakein – **Alan Lakein** was a best-selling author on time management, who wrote *How to Get Control of Your Time and Your Life* which has sold over 3 million copies. Across our timeline of strategic changes that we would bring into existence, there is a constant mingling of the past, present, and future. The ability to move our focus among these three realities heightens our ability to manifest the most positive outcome with relationship to each. A key to accessing this ability is to imagine outside of the constrictions of time, space, and personality; a metaphysical modality.

10. "Reduce your plan to writing. The moment you complete this, you will have definitely given concrete form to the

intangible desire." – Napoleon Hill –    Many of us know Napoleon Hill for his 17 Principles of Success and his best-selling books *The Law of Success* (1928) and *Think and Grow Rich* (1937), which have sold more than 20 million copies. He is considered as one of most important modern pioneers in the success and personal achievement movement.  Hill's words of instruction are particularly taken to heart by this author.  This very book is concrete evidence of my belief in the power of committing your visionary intentions to writing.

Wow!  I wish I had said each of these powerful affirmations of duty to planning and success.  Once I think about it, I have repeated these empowering statements herein, committed them to writing, and will likely read them again and again over the seasons, years, and decades ahead.  Smart, huh?

# Time to Get Your Hustle On

*"This life is yours. Take the power to choose what you want to do and do it well. Take the power to love what you want in life and love it honestly. Take the power to walk in the forest and be a part of nature. Take the power to control your own life. No one else can do it for you. Take the power to make your life happy."*
— Susan Polis Schutz

## Suffering for the Errors of My Youth

I have long considered myself a proper hustler, a go-getter, and someone willing to go the extra mile to achieve key goals related to personal and professional success.

Hell, who did I think that I was fooling? I believed, and many people confirmed that I was a fairly competent researcher and writer. Still, I never had been able to crack consistent book sales. Sure, when I attended conventions or conferences I did comparatively well; better than many others that shared the same space.

Looking back, I know now that I was always held back because I lacked a team that was as willing as me to get these books to market. Even when I was married, the wife never saw a value in what I was publishing. To the contrary, I realize now that she resented my writing career, blaming my publishing ambitions for stealing my attention away from strictly chasing the dollars that had once been flowing like a strong and steady river when we first got together.

If I had the chance to live the last three decades all over, this book *The Art of the Book Hustle* should have been written at that time – especially as I was naturally directed to do this as a *solopreneur*. As I have the luxury of 20/20 hindsight, I see that not learning how to engage the spectrum of marketing techniques that are the subject of this book was my main failure to succeed fully in this arena. I've learned from my big mistakes.

Reading this book, you do not have to make these same errors. To the best of your abilities, break out of the "lone wolf" syndrome and assemble a team of competent people that can assist your mission. Get used to the fact that you will have to invest 20% or more of your gross revenues in marketing. Put the right people, experienced players, into a position to assist your vision. Do this as early in your writing career as possible.

Once you have assembled a reasonable team, get to work – plan your work and work your plan. These insights that I share herein will be most rewarding.

## Get Started with Your Hustler's Strategic Action Plan

As a writer and an independent book publisher, you can utilize multiple low-cost strategies to increase your book sales. Here are 25 such strategies that you can consider:

1.  **Leverage social media platforms**: Use social media platforms like Twitter, Facebook, Instagram, and LinkedIn to promote your book and connect with potential readers.

2.  **Build an author website**: Create an author website where readers can learn more about your book and purchase it online.

3. **Optimize your book's metadata**: Optimize your book's title, subtitle, description, and keywords to make it more discoverable on online bookstores.

4. **Encourage readers to leave reviews** of your book on Amazon, Goodreads, and other book review sites.

5. **Run a Goodreads give-away**: Host a give-away on Goodreads to increase visibility and generate interest in your book.

6. **Create a book trailer**: Create a short video trailer for your book and share it on social media platforms and your author website.

7. **Offer free content**: Create free content related to your book, such as blog posts, whitepapers, or webinars, to attract potential readers.

8. **Utilize email marketing**: Build an email list of potential readers and send them targeted marketing messages about your book.

9. **Leverage book clubs**: Reach out to book clubs and offer them a discount on your book to encourage group purchases.

10. **Create champions for leading book clubs**, galvanize people in their geographical location, promote and help market.

11. **Participate in book fairs and festivals**: Attend book fairs and festivals to showcase your book and connect with potential readers.

12. **Create a study curriculum** for the distinct body of wisdom.

13. **Partner with influencers**: Partner with influencers in your niche or genre to promote your book to their followers.

14. **Run a Facebook or Instagram ad campaign**: Use Facebook or Instagram advertising to target potential readers with ads for your book.

15. **Utilize Amazon advertising**: Use Amazon advertising to promote your book on Amazon and increase visibility.

16. **Offer a discount or promotion**: Offer a limited-time discount or promotion to encourage readers to purchase your book.

17. **Participate in online book communities**: Participate in online book communities, such as Goodreads groups or Facebook book clubs, to connect with potential readers.

18. **Host a book launch event**: Host a virtual or in-person book launch event to generate excitement and buzz around your book.

19. **Reach out to book bloggers**: Reach out to book bloggers in your niche or genre and offer them a free copy of your book in exchange for a review.

20. **Offer a book bundle**: Bundle your book with other books in your genre to encourage readers to purchase multiple books at once.

21. **Leverage local media**: Reach out to local media outlets, such as newspapers or radio stations, to get coverage for your book.

22. **Participate in book-related hashtags**: Participate in book-related hashtags on social media platforms to connect with potential readers.

23. **Offer a free sample**: Offer a free sample of your book, such as a free chapter or excerpt, to encourage readers to purchase the full book.

24. **Leverage word of mouth**: Encourage readers to share your book with their friends and family to increase visibility.

25. **Utilize book discovery platforms**: Use book discovery platforms, such as BookBub or Goodreads, to increase

visibility and generate interest in your book. Later in this book I will share a list of what Kindlepreneur considers the best book promo sites.

26. **Participate in author interviews**: Participate in author interviews on podcasts or blogs to increase visibility and generate interest in your book.

27. **Create an author newsletter**: Create an author newsletter to keep your readers updated on your writing and new book releases.

We've shared a reasonably-sized list of tasks that will get you into action. Return on investment for these strategies will likely propel you to a new level of energy, confidence, and emotional engagement. Your momentum will gradually build as you learn to make these actions practical and habitual. You will certainly separate yourself from the crowd. You will unleash the beast in your writing and publishing potential.

# Important Components of a Book to Consider

*Get up early in the morning. Taking charge of your lifestyle and schedule now. Adapt to the lifestyle of an entrepreneur with taking ownership of your schedule. If you don't do that now, you will have a really hard time making the transition.*
— Dave Chesson, Founder of Kindlepreneur

It has taken many years of hands-on experience to discover the practicality of including the following authoring components. I trust that you will find these satisfyingly practical.

## Front Matter

**What is front matter?** – Front matter in book writing refers to the preliminary pages found at the beginning of a book before the main content. It includes elements like the title page, copyright page, table of contents, dedication, preface, and acknowledgments. Front matter provides essential information about the book, its author, and its structure. It helps readers navigate the content and understand the context before delving into the book's main body.

**Half-title page** – A half-title page is a simple page that usually displays only the book's main title, often centered and at the top. It appears before the title page and provides a minimalist introduction to the book's title, serving as a transition between the cover and the full title page. While it lacks additional information like subtitles or author names, it helps set the tone and anticipation for the reader before they proceed to the formal beginning of the book.

**Copyright page** – A copyright page is a crucial element located on one of the early pages of a book. It contains essential legal and bibliographic information, including the copyright notice, publication date, ISBN or other identification numbers, information about the publisher, printing details, and sometimes legal disclaimers. The copyright page ensures proper attribution, protects intellectual property rights, and provides readers with key information about the book's publication and distribution.

**Title page** – A title page is the initial page that presents fundamental details about the book. It typically includes the full book title and the author's name, often accompanied by a subtitle. The title page may also display the publisher's name, logo, city, and year of publication. It serves as a visual introduction to the book's content and establishes its identity while providing essential information for identification and reference purposes.

**Dedication page** – A dedication page is a space where authors express their sentiments or gratitude by dedicating their work to a specific person, group, or cause. It's usually a brief statement located at the beginning of the book, often on its own page. This page allows authors to honor individuals who have been important in their lives or played a significant role in the book's creation. It adds a personal touch and establishes emotional connections with readers.

**Table of contents (TOC)** – A TOC is a list of a book's major sections, chapters, and often subsections, along with the corresponding page numbers. It serves as a roadmap for readers, providing a structured overview of the book's organization and content. This navigational tool helps readers locate specific topics, chapters, or information quickly, enhancing their reading experience by facilitating easy access to different parts of the book without the need to read linearly from cover to cover.

**Foreword** – A foreword is a short introductory piece typically written by someone other than the author, such as a notable figure, expert, or colleague. It appears at the beginning of the book and provides context, insights, or endorsements that help set the stage for the reader. A foreword offers an external perspective on the book's significance, the author's credentials, or the book's subject matter, often adding credibility and depth to the reader's understanding of the work.

**Preface** – A preface is an author-written introduction at the start of a book. It explains the author's purpose, motivations, and the circumstances surrounding the book's creation. Unlike a foreword, a preface is authored by the book's writer and provides insight into the book's origins, methodology, or personal connection to the subject matter. It offers readers a glimpse into the author's intentions and provides context that enhances their understanding of the book's content and significance.

**Epigraph** – An epigraph is a brief quotation, phrase, or excerpt from another source that appears at the beginning of a book, chapter, or section. It sets the tone, provides thematic context, or offers insights into the following content. An epigraph can come from literature, philosophy, or any relevant field, and its selection is a deliberate choice made by the author to enhance the reader's understanding of the book's themes or to establish a specific mood.

## Body Text

**Prologue** – A prologue is an introductory section that appears before the main narrative of a story. It provides important background information, context, or events that took place before the main story begins. A prologue can offer insights into the story's setting, characters, or overarching themes, helping to engage the reader and set the stage for the main plot. It often aims to pique curiosity and create anticipation for the unfolding narrative.

**Main body** – The main body is the core section of the book that contains the primary content, narrative, or exposition. It encompasses the central themes, plot development, character interactions, and the presented primary ideas or arguments. In fiction, it includes the unfolding of the story's events and character arcs. In non-fiction, it comprises a detailed exploration of the book's subject matter. The main body constitutes the substantial portion of the book where the core messages and storytelling occur.

**Epilogue** – An epilogue is a concluding section that comes after the main narrative of a story. It provides closure, insights, or a glimpse into what happens to the characters or the story's world after the main events have concluded. An epilogue can tie up loose ends, offer reflections on the story's themes, or provide a sense of resolution. It allows readers to reflect on the story's implications and the characters' futures.

## Back Matter

**Afterword** – An afterword is a commentary or reflection added by the author or another relevant individual appearing at the book's end. It provides insights, context, or additional information about the book's creation, subject matter, or significance. Unlike a preface, which appears at the beginning, an afterword offers perspectives after the main content. It can include personal anecdotes, updates, or thoughts on the book's impact, enriching the reader's understanding and connection to the work.

**Book glossary** – A book glossary is a section at the end of a book, usually before the index, that lists and defines specialized or technical terms used in the book's content. It provides readers with a reference point to understand unfamiliar terminology, enhancing their comprehension of the subject matter. A glossary is particularly common in textbooks, academic works, or books dealing with complex topics, helping readers navigate and grasp the specialized language used throughout the book.

**Book discussion questions** – Book discussion questions encourage deeper engagement and critical thinking among readers. They prompt thoughtful conversations and analysis about the book's themes, characters, plot, and messages. These questions can facilitate book club discussions, classroom activities, or individual reflection, enhancing the overall reading experience. By addressing different aspects of the book, discussion questions foster a deeper understanding of its content and encourage readers to share diverse interpretations and perspectives.

**Book appendix** – An appendix is a supplementary section at the end of a book containing additional information, data, references, or materials that support or expand upon the main content. It includes details relevant to a subset of readers but not essential to the main narrative. Appendices can include charts, graphs, tables, documents, or extended explanations that offer in-depth information without interrupting the flow of the main text.

**Chronology** – A chronology is a chronological listing or timeline of events presented in the order in which they occurred. It provides readers with a clear and organized overview of the sequence of events, helping them understand the progression of a story, historical developments, or other related occurrences. Chronologies are often used in historical, biographical, or non-fiction works to enhance readers' comprehension of the timeline and relationships between different events in the narrative.

**Character guide** – A character guide is a reference section that provides detailed information about the characters in the story. It typically includes descriptions of each character's physical appearance, personality traits, background, motivations, and roles within the narrative. A character guide helps readers keep track of the various characters and their relationships, especially in complex stories with numerous individuals. It enhances the reading experience by offering insights into the characters' development and significance.

**Additional information** – The purpose of including additional information is to enrich the reader's understanding and experience. This supplementary content, such as appendices, glossaries, maps, or references, offers in-depth insights, clarifications, or context related to the main content. It caters to different readers' needs, providing tools for research, clarification of terms, or visual aids. By offering these resources, authors enhance the book's value, making it more accessible, informative, and engaging for a diverse range of readers.

**Book acknowledgments** – The purpose of book acknowledgments is to express the author's gratitude to individuals or entities who contributed support, guidance, or inspiration during the writing and publishing process. Acknowledgments recognize the efforts of editors, mentors, family, friends, or researchers who assisted in various capacities. They offer a personal touch, showing appreciation for the collaborative effort that goes into creating a book. Acknowledgments also build connections between the author and readers, conveying the social and collaborative aspects of writing. Often, this is placed in the front matter section.

**About the author** – This section provides information about the author's background, accomplishments, and expertise. It offers insights into the author's qualifications, which can lend credibility to their written content. This section helps readers understand the author's perspective and motivation for writing the book, fostering a connection between the author and the readers. It also serves as a promotional tool, introducing the author to potential readers and building their reputation. This often appears on the back inside cover of hardcover books.

**Book accolades** – Publishers include book accolades, such as reviews, endorsements, or awards, to showcase the book's quality, appeal, and recognition within the literary community. These accolades serve as endorsements from experts or respected figures, influencing potential readers' perception of the book's value. Positive reviews and awards can attract more attention, boost sales, and build the book's reputation. Including accolades on book covers or marketing materials helps establish credibility and encourages readers to explore the work further.

**Bibliography** – Publishers include a bibliography to provide readers with a list of sources and references used by the author during research or inspiration. It verifies the book's credibility and demonstrates the thoroughness of the author's work. The bibliography allows interested readers to delve deeper into the subject matter by exploring the sources mentioned. It also offers transparency and accountability, showing that the book's content is well-informed and based on reliable information.

**Index** — It is wise to include an index to enhance the book's usability and accessibility. An index compiles keywords, terms, and topics discussed in the book, along with corresponding page numbers. It allows readers to quickly locate specific information, aiding research, reference, and navigation. A well-structured index streamlines readers' engagement, making it easier to find relevant content, enhancing the overall reading experience, and ensuring the book is a valuable resource for both casual readers and researchers.

There you have it. Now, you know so much more about key components that you can include in your book to make it more relevant, navigable, credible, and *awesome*. I hope this helps.

# Proven Strategies to Increase Sales

*"My theory on life is that life is beautiful. Life doesn't change. You have a day, and a night, and a month, and a year. We people change – we can be miserable or we can be happy. It's what you make of your life."*
– Mohammed bin Rashid Al Maktoum

## If It Were Easy, Then Everyone Would Do It, Right?

How have the most prosperous independent book authors and publishers been able to increase their sales using marketing and promotion strategies? – The answer to that question is as complex as one could imagine, and this book will strive to illustrate this very point; there are many components to consider.

To match the most successful independents, you and I must put in extra work. My ambition for decades has been to generate the level of book sales that will allow me to achieve "a normal life." I want to pay my bills on time and have money to spare at the end of each monthly cycle of expenses. I want to have surplus to buy nice gifts for my children and grandchildren.

Yet, success and failure are often best understood when broken down into the simplest elements. To simplify this, one can say that profitable booksellers do everything within their spectrum of talents and abilities to achieve a supreme focus on success – ultimately, they succeed.

The most successful independent authors and book publishers have used various marketing and promotion strategies to increase sales. Here are some approaches that have proven effective:

## Building an author platform

Successful independent authors often focus on building their personal brand and establishing an online presence. They utilize websites, blogs, social media platforms, and email newsletters to engage with their readers, share updates, and promote their work.

## Engaging with the target audience

Understanding and connecting with the target audience is crucial. Successful authors interact with their readers through social media, forums, and events, fostering relationships and building a loyal fan base. They respond to comments, participate in discussions, and seek feedback to improve their work.

Buyers are commonly convinced by these three marketing strategies: *emotional appeal*, *reasoning logic*, and *the scarcity principle*. Let's look deeper into how these strong sentiments have become so predictably usable when wielded by experienced marketers.

## The Power of Emotional Appeal in Marketing

In the vast landscape of modern marketing, a fundamental truth remains unwavering: emotions wield an unparalleled influence over consumer behavior. As businesses strive to captivate their audiences and carve a lasting niche in a competitive marketplace, they recognize the potent allure of appealing to emotions. This subchapter explores how marketers harness the compelling force of emotions to forge strong connections, drive purchasing decisions, and cultivate brand loyalty.

Human emotions are a complex tapestry of feelings that shape our perceptions, decisions, and experiences. Marketers adeptly navigate this emotional terrain by crafting narratives that resonate deeply with their target audience. They create a relatable and empathetic bond between consumers and brands by tapping into universal emotions like joy, fear, love, and nostalgia. For instance, an advertisement depicting a heartwarming family reunion or an inspiring underdog story captures one's attention and triggers a sense of sentimental belonging. Successful emotional engagement can foster a long-lasting affinity, making customers more receptive to a brand's offerings.

Emotions not only capture attention but also drive purchasing decisions. Neuroscientific research reveals that strong emotional stimuli elicit reactive responses in the brain, enhancing heightened memory retention. Marketers strategically exploit this phenomenon, ensuring their campaigns leave an indelible mark in consumers' minds. An emotionally resonant advertisement can trigger a subconscious association, prompting individuals to choose a particular product or service amidst many options. Apple's iconic "Think Different" campaign, which appealed to the desire for innovation and individuality, "transformed its products into symbols of creativity and ingenuity," resulting in unprecedented customer loyalty.

Furthermore, emotional connections foster brand loyalty and advocacy. Consumers who feel emotionally connected to a brand are likelier to become its advocates, spreading positive word-of-mouth and influencing their social circles. Marketers can create a community of loyal brand ambassadors by cultivating a sense of shared values or aligning with consumers' aspirations. Recall Nike's "Just Do It" slogan. Coupled with emotionally charged narratives of athletes overcoming challenges, it boosted sales and inspired a movement that celebrates determination and perseverance. All accomplished with three simple words.

In conclusion, the art of selling through emotional appeal is a cornerstone of modern marketing strategies. By tapping into the wellspring of human emotions, marketers create powerful narratives that resonate with consumers, drive purchasing decisions, and foster brand loyalty. As consumers seek authentic and meaningful connections, mastering emotional appeal remains essential for marketers to forge lasting bonds in an ever-evolving marketplace.

## The Logic of Effective Marketing: Appeal to Reason

In the dynamic marketing realm, the ability to persuade through logical reasoning has emerged as a cornerstone strategy for businesses seeking to capture the minds of consumers. While emotions can play a compelling role, appealing to logic offers a distinct avenue for marketers to connect with their target audience. This essay delves into how marketers leverage rationality and logical persuasion to influence consumer behavior, shape perceptions, and drive informed decision-making.

Logic is a potent tool that resonates deeply with consumers who prioritize facts, data, and rational analysis when making purchasing choices. Marketers capitalize on this by presenting compelling arguments backed by evidence, research, and statistics. By demonstrating the practical benefits, features, and advantages of a product or service, they provide consumers with a clear understanding of how their offering addresses specific needs or problems. For instance, a technology company might emphasize its latest laptop's processing speed, storage capacity, and security features, catering to consumers who seek a logical justification for their investment.

Moreover, logical persuasion instills a sense of trust and credibility. In an era where information overload and skepticism abound, consumers value transparency and reliability. By offering well-structured, fact-based content, marketers position themselves as experts who prioritize customer well-being. This approach not only garners initial interest but also paves the way for enduring customer relationships built on trust. For instance, a pharmaceutical company might employ clinical trial results and expert endorsements to convey the effectiveness and safety of a new medication, assuaging concerns and generating confidence.

Furthermore, logic appeals to the innate desire for value and utility. Consumers seek products and services that align with their practical needs and provide a tangible return on investment. Marketers adeptly showcase how their offerings offer solutions that deliver measurable results. A cleaning product advertisement, for instance, may emphasize its superior stain-removing capabilities and cost-effectiveness, appealing to consumers' most practical considerations.

In conclusion, the strategic use of logical reasoning in marketing offers a compelling approach to engage and influence consumers. Marketers tap into the rational decision-making processes that guide consumer choices by providing evidence-based insights, establishing trust, and highlighting practical benefits. In an era of informed consumers, the ability to present a compelling logical case can be the differentiator that sways decisions and fosters lasting brand loyalty.

## The Art of Scarcity: Drive Demand Through Exclusivity

In the intricate dance of marketing, scarcity has emerged as a captivating strategy that arouses intrigue and compels consumers to take action. The principle is simple yet powerful: marketers ignite a sense of urgency and exclusivity that drives demand for products and services by creating an illusion of limited availability. This subchapter delves into how marketers leverage the scarcity principle to captivate audiences, stimulate desire, enhance a brand's allure, and drive sales.

Scarcity taps into a fundamental psychological trigger—*fear of missing out* (FOMO). Marketers adeptly employ this emotion to create a sense of urgency, urging consumers to act swiftly before an opportunity slips away. By using phrases like "limited edition," "exclusive offer," or "while supplies last," marketers instill a fear that they might miss out on a unique experience or product, prompting consumers to make impulsive purchasing decisions. For instance, a fashion brand might release a limited quantity of a new clothing line, leveraging scarcity to generate a flurry of purchases driven by the desire to own a piece of the coveted collection.

Additionally, scarcity elevates the perceived value of a product or service. When something is rare or hard to obtain, it becomes more desirable and sought after. Marketers play on this psychological tendency by creating a perception of high demand and low supply. This prompts consumers to assign greater value to the item, often justifying a higher price point. Luxury brands masterfully employ this strategy, positioning their products as symbols of prestige and exclusivity that only a privileged few will attain.

Scarcity also fosters a sense of loyalty and commitment among consumers. When individuals invest time, effort, or resources to secure a scarce item, they connect with the brand more deeply. This emotional investment enhances brand loyalty and encourages repeat purchases, as consumers associate the brand with their successful quest for something rare and special.

In conclusion, scarcity is a potent marketing tool that taps into fundamental human psychology to drive demand and create a sense of urgency. By invoking FOMO, elevating perceived value, and fostering emotional connections, marketers effectively leverage scarcity to captivate audiences and stimulate consumer action. As consumers continue to seek unique and exclusive experiences, the strategic use of scarcity remains a compelling strategy that shapes modern marketing landscapes.

## Leveraging book reviews and endorsements

Positive reviews and endorsements can significantly boost sales. Successful authors actively seek reviews from reputable book bloggers, influencers, and industry professionals. They may offer free copies of their book to generate reviews or seek endorsements from established authors in their genre.

## Utilizing effective book covers and blurbs

A visually appealing and professionally designed book cover can attract potential readers. Successful authors invest in a high-quality cover design that accurately represents their book's genre and content. They also craft compelling blurbs that grab readers' attention and entice them to explore further.

## Employing targeted online advertising

Paid online advertising, such as social media ads and search engine marketing, can effectively reach a specific audience.

Successful authors carefully identify their target audience and create targeted ad campaigns to promote their books. They monitor the performance of these ads and make adjustments as necessary.

## Utilizing book promotion sites and newsletters

Various websites and newsletters cater specifically to book promotion. Successful authors leverage these platforms to feature their books, reach new readers, and generate sales. Some popular examples include BookBub, Ereader News Today, and The Fussy Librarian.

## Offering promotions and discounts

Limited-time promotions, discounted pricing, or offering the first book in a series for free can encourage readers to try a new author. Successful authors strategically use these tactics to capture attention, generate buzz, and ultimately increase sales. They may promote these offers through their website, social media, newsletters, and targeted advertising.

## Participating in book signings and events

In-person interactions with readers can be invaluable. Successful authors attend book signings, literary festivals, conventions, and other relevant events to meet readers, sign books, and create personal connections. These events help raise awareness of their work and can lead to word-of-mouth recommendations.

## Collaborating with other authors

Collaboration with fellow authors can expand an author's reach. Successful authors participate in joint promotions, bundle their books, or co-author projects with other authors in their genre. This cross-promotion exposes their work to a wider audience and should result in increased sales.

# Continuously improving writing and editing

Quality writing is crucial for sustained success. Successful authors strive to improve their writing skills by seeking feedback from beta readers, joining writing groups, attending workshops, and hiring professional editors. They understand the importance of producing well-crafted, error-free books that meet readers' expectations.

It's worth noting that the effectiveness of marketing and promotion strategies can vary based on factors such as genre, target audience, budget, and individual author preferences. Experimentation and adaptation to the evolving publishing landscape are essential for long-term success in the independent author and book publishing industry. Most successful independent authors and book publishers have increased their sales through marketing and promotional strategies.

# Teaching Online Courses

Each book you have authored might be considered a separate online teaching course. An ambitious author could launch a course a month using one or more of the following platforms:

- **ThinkIFC**, Score 8.3 out of 10 – https://www.thinkific.com
  Free / $36 month / $74 month / $149 month / Accelerator Program $499

- **LearnWorlds**, – https://www.learnworlds.com
  Starter $24 / Pro $79 / Learning Center $249 / High Volume

- **LearnDash**, Score 9.2 out of 10 - https://www.learndash.com
  Add to WordPress Starter $25 month / Plugins $199 year

- **TeachAble**, Score 8.3 out of 10 – https://teachable.com/
  Free / Basic $39 month / Pro $119 month

- **Udemy**, Score 8.4 out of 10 –
  https://www.udemy.com/teaching/
  Pricing cloud $360 per year

- **Skillshare**, Ratings 3.7 out of 5 stars -
  https://www.skillshare.com/

- **Podia**, Score 8.6 out of 10 - https://www.podia.com/
  Free / Mover $33 month / Shaker $75 month

- **Kajabi**, Score 8.5 out of 10 - https://kajabi.com/
  Basic $149 month / Growth $199 month / Pro $399 month

- **Mighty Networks** - https://www.mightynetworks.com/
  Community $39 month / Business $119 month / Mighty Pro

- **Simplero** - https://simplero.com
  Starter $59 month / Scale $149 month / Skyrocket $249 month

- **TrainerCentral** - https://www.trainercentral.com/
  Free / Starter $20 / Pro $50 month

- **Gumroad** Ratings 3 out of 5 stars- https://gumroad.com/
  Pricing 10% flat rate

- **Coursify** – https://coursify.me/
  Free; Pro $29 month / Business $59

In theory, each book title could support a distinct class. With this being my 52nd published book, I could switch to teaching online as a full-time profession… Hmmmm?

Web learning companies offer thousands of courses that have enrolled millions of students in learning more about subjects specific to their passions, interests, needs, and crafts.

## Create a Landing Page for Your Book Funnel

Rather than waste the target audience's time searching through a website, get them to a landing page for the book that has grabbed their attention as directly as possible.

This landing page can offer them a direct means of purchasing the item of their interest. As well, it can also conveniently create an "upselling" opportunity, which can further steer them to related books, services, or merchandise with several other deals available from the landing page.

Here are several tips to make your landing page more effective toward getting the results that you desire:

1.  **Keep it simple**, clean, and well-organized;

2.  Use a **powerful header** to highlight the offer value;

3.  Be sure to **align your ad copy with the headline**;

4.  Be sure to align your offer with the **right target audience**;

5.  Create distinctive **landing pages for individual audiences**;

6.  Make sure that your promotion **appeals to the audience's emotions, logic, and "scarcity"**;

7.  Keep in mind that the landing page's **highest priority is to convert visits** into real prospects;

8.  Feature clearly defined **calls-to-action**;

9.  Keep a **tight focus on the highest priorities** that accomplish the tasks that close the deal;

10. Keep in mind that this is not all about your business priorities, and **keep the customer central** to the communication;

11. Make proper use of **"trust signals"** that communicate that your brand and offers are trustworthy;

12. Make sure that your landing page is **friendly for mobile device users**;

13. Keep it **simple, short, and a quick-read**;

14. Keep in mind that a good landing page should **satisfy the visitor and not require them to go elsewhere** to research to confirm the value of your offers further;

15. Be sure to **address any anxieties** that your customers might feel;

16. Ask for just the **right amount of information from the user,** and don't overwhelm them with too extensive of a survey;

17. Properly design for **good graphics, colors, and cleanliness**;

18. Incorporate the idea of **speed into the browsing experience** and be sure that your landing page loads quickly;

19. Keep in mind the user's strong desire for **safety and security**;

20. Thoroughly **test your landing page links before launching** because once it is out there, there's no recalling it and apologizing for bad links;

21. **Properly use analytics** to see that your offers meet your intended goals.

# Great Insights from Kindlepreneur

*"I don't hold back at all. My goal with every article or video is to give you everything you need to know so that you can turn around and take action, and see results. I hope for this to be a compendium of self publishing and book marketing knowledge so that real authors can get their books seen."* – Dave Chesson

## Print-on-Demand: The Book Hustler's New Tool

I have been publishing and printing my books for several years through Kindle Direct Publishing's print-on-demand service. This is about the fifth printing service that I have used over the past thirty years. I began using copy shops and moved through two printers that did large runs of my books (that had to be paid in full upon delivery – sometimes running thousands of dollars). At that time, I switched to *48-Hour Books*, an excellent Ohio-based printer that did smaller runs of 100-500 books at a time; the larger the print order, the higher the markup for each book. As an independent publisher, I was constrained by having to order such large print orders and pay shipping across the country.

About ten years ago, in the mid-2010s, I discovered the convenience of print-on-demand. The first advantage was that I could print much smaller quantities of each title while still keeping the book cost very low. Compared to the previous printer, the price for each printed copy at a purchase of five books was equivalent to my costs to print two hundred or more. Another great advantage was the problem of storing hundreds of books until they were sold. As I got to the point that I had more than twenty titles in print, as you can easily imagine, my storage problem was demanding.

Today, I have become quite a fan of print-on-demand (POD). Because of this valuable service, I have seen several advantages:

- I can order small-size print runs that arrive at my office within 6-14 days on average;

- Inventory storage equals capital stagnation. If I have hundreds or thousands of books warehoused in my garage, that represents money that is unused and not accessible until those books are sold;

- The cost-per-copy of POD is equivalent to what I would have to buy books by the hundreds to achieve with traditional printing houses;

- When using traditional printing houses, I had to wait days or incur large mailing fees to get a "galley print," which is a look at the final print that can expose needed changes if the book is not correct. With POD, I can see a finished copy of the book by buying it retail on the day of availability. This saves me time and money, as it also gets the book in the active marketplace much quicker.

- With POD, and using Amazon's international reach, I can order books in other world markets for customers in those regions. This has most often eliminated the huge postal fees incurred when I ship from the U.S. to buyers in the U.K., Eurozone, Canada, Mexico, or Asia, where my readers are mostly located;

- With the publication of **The Art of the Book Hustle**, I will now have 46 books in active print. I can thus store 10-15 copies in my office rather than dozens or hundreds of copies of the books in the garage and around the house;

- For books that are not big sellers, POD allows me to have them in inventory without spending more than the small investment needed for just a few copies at the publisher's discounted cost;

- After the book is in hand, I can make needed changes to the content or artwork, which will be uploaded to the printer and will be available in a couple of days for the marketplace.

For these reasons and more, switching to print-on-demand has proven a significant advantage to my success as a writer-publisher. For other independents, you will not regret making this move as you further develop your publishing industry crafts.

## Insights on Building Book Sales from Kindlepreneur

Once a writer is registered with Kindle Direct Publishing, they offer a broad set of tools, insights, reports, and user experiences that will serve to the great advantage to the book hustler. I will admit to having procrastinated looking closer at these marketing tips and tools shared by KDP. Much of my hesitance is the challenges of being too busy with daily scheduling and my primary passion as a writer more than a marketing publisher.

With the commitment to this book, the increased focus on increasing daily book sales has forced me to look at the available tools that will accomplish the goals listed herein. I *commit* to mastering The Art of the Book Hustle – I need *more gain* with *no shame*!

Yesterday, I got an email from KDP with powerful information in it. It seems as if I am recently being treated like a VIP by KDP, likely due to my huge output as a non-fiction writer and publisher. If it is true, I appreciate their acknowledgment of how hard I am trying to become a best-selling author.

So, this time, I opened the email and spent a few hours browsing through the Kindlepreneur insights, even sharing them during my morning Internet radio broadcast. Based upon a day's worth of grabbing these insights from **Kindlepreneur**, let's look at some of the main insights.

## Amazon Kindle Rankings

The key to selling your Kindle eBook is getting it in front of the most potential customers. Some authors do this with elaborate launches, extensive pre-developed email lists, and other cutting-edge tactics. However, many Kindle authors neglect the simple optimization of their eBook sales page on Amazon.

By making some simple word changes and tweaking your Amazon product page, you can dramatically increase your Amazon rankings. You can also show up for more Amazon searches, therefore getting your eBook in front of your potential customers more often.

If you're not sure how to do that, don't worry. This guide will show you exactly how you can take actionable steps to improve your Amazon rankings and get your eBook in front of more customers, which means more sales and more money for you.

The best part about this is that each step is completely free and can be completed within a couple of hours.

Critical points made within this report include:

- **Be Responsible and Moral** – Don't use this information deceptively. Don't spam readers with useless, pointless keywords that are only clickbait. In the long run, this will backfire.

- **Algorithms and Search Engines** – Much of search engine optimization (SEO) works from automated apps. This section shows how to use these most impactfully.

- **Number of Verified Reviews** – Getting people to read and review your book is a powerful means of increasing your rankings in the Amazon book search process. These tips include searching for similar books and using websites like GoodReads to find authors that could be encouraged to review your book gift. Be careful to avoid *trolls* who review a lot of books negatively. You can also get friends and other writers you've worked with to exchange reviews with you.

- **Number of Sales** – Amazon's main purpose is to generate sales. Books that sell more will rise higher in the rankings that select searched books. If you can put the right keywords into place, your book will place higher, yet your past sales numbers will have an impact. More recent sales carry higher weight than older sales. Also, free books will not be more recommended than books for sale. You can strategically use free books for a while, then switch to a paid-for strategy after generating buzz.

- **Click-Through Rate (CTR)** – Okay, you have developed successful strategies to get your book noticed, but that doesn't necessarily mean that you will be selected among the search selections. Improving the CTR rate is thus an important area to focus your strategic planning.

- **Choose the Right Keywords** – SEO is directly linked to the keywords associated with your book. In multiple ways, keywords carry much weight on how your text will be noticed. Obviously, keywords, SEO, description of your book, and other factors will go a long way to get your book out of a search result and into someone's library.

## Trigger Words for Books

Use these trigger words to increase the power of your book title and description. This increases the strength of your book's page, making readers more likely to purchase.

However, to read your book's page, shoppers must find it in the Amazon store first. To increase the number of views on your book's page, improve your seven keyword boxes.

Improve their effectivity (and therefore the number of eyes on your book) by using these strategies for fiction or nonfiction.

The following are some of the most impactful *emotional words* used for various categories associated with promoting and marketing your written works. Here is a selection of the words suggested by Kindlepreneur that marketers and authors can use to trigger an emotional association within the potential reader's mind that will increase the likelihood of sales.

- **Selling** – authentic, best-selling, endorsed, guaranteed, money back, no obligation, no risk, protected, recession-proof, results, tested, unconditional;

- **Romance** – crave, depraved, desire, dirty, explicit, forbidden, lonely, lust, naked, passionate, promiscuous, scandalous, sensual, sex, shameless, sinful, sleazy, steamy, taboo tantalizing, tease, uncensored, wild;

- **Energy (vibrance)** – amazing, awe-inspiring, breathtaking, daring, epic, excited, fearless, guts, jaw-dropping, legendary, mind-blowing, relentless, sensational, spectacular, staggering, surprising, uplifting, victory, wonderful;

- **Fear** – annihilate, Armageddon, assault, beware, bloodbath, cataclysmic, catastrophe, chilling, corpse, crazy, crisis, danger, deadly, debilitating, destroy, devastating, disastrous, epidemic, frightening, hazardous, hoax, holocaust, horrific, invasion, lunatic, mistake, murder, nightmare, painful, panic, plague, poison, revenge, savage, slaughter, sociopath, terror, torture, toxic, victim, vulnerable, wounded;

- **Trust** – accredited, approved, authentic, best-selling, certified, fully refundable, guaranteed, ironclad, no obligation, no risk, no strings attached, official, proven, recession-proof, refund, reliable, research, secure, tested, verify, unconditional, well respected;

- **Anger** – arrogant, backstabbing, BS, coward, disgusting, foul, hostile, lies, moneygrubbing, morally bankrupt, obnoxious, revolting, ruthless, stuck up, thug, underhanded;

- **Greed** – bargain, bonus, cash, cheap, discount, economical, fortune, free, frugal, gift, giveaway, inexpensive, jackpot, marked down, massive, monetize, money, price break, profit, reduced, rich, savings, six-figure, soaring, treasure, up-sell, value;

- **Mystery** – banned, behind the scenes, black market, blacklisted, censored, classified, concealed, confessions, confidential, controversial, covert, cover-up, forbidden, hidden, illegal, insider, little known, off-limits, outlawed, priceless, private, restricted, secrets, smuggled, strange, trade secret, unauthorized, underground, withheld.

You might want to add your own emotion-triggering words to these extensive lists. Also, combining these words and the feelings that they emote could go a long way toward creating just the right book title, subtitle, marketing slogan, or media appearance that will compel the widest audience possible. This is all about creativity and your ability to project your intellectual prowess. I am quite impressed with this set of insights from Kindlepreneur.

## Best Book Promo Websites

The following sites suggested by Kindlepreneur have multiple options. They can range from free to thousands of dollars. They also have various-sized email databases, social media integration, a large spread in monthly traffic, and Alexa rankings.

- **Awesome Gang** – The only one on this shared list that offers a free option, it does have other options for only $10, making it the low-entry member of this group.

- **Bknights Fiverr /Digital Book Spot** – The low price point of $5 - $10 makes this an easy entry point. Not much is said by the compiler of this list, Dave Chesson, about its effective reach.

- **BookBub** – This has a much broader price range from $21 to over $3000, offering much greater market penetration through emails and social media. Amazon's Alexa ranks this the highest of this group of book promo sites, and it boasts the most increased monthly traffic of all listed sites.

- **BookSends** – Costs for services range from $50 - $250, and its range of services seems to cater to smaller-scale independents.

- **Books Butterfly** – With prices ranging from $90 - $400, it has what appears to be mid-level access and reach. It appears to have the lowest level of monthly traffic on the list, which could be advantageous if it applies to highly motivated niche readers.

- **Ereader News Today** – Another book promo site to appeal for those on a smaller budget with offerings ranging from $45 - $150. Alexa ranks it fifth on this list of ten promo sites.

- **FKBT - Free Kindle Books & Tips** – Judging by the name we can assume that it is associated with the Amazon group and KDP books. Pricing is in the low range from $25 - $125. Amazon's own Alexa ranks it seventh on this list of ten promo sites.

- **Free Booksy** – I have used Booksly for a number of resources in recent years regarding my book authoring course. Their paid services range between $30 - $200, in contrast to the free stuff. I have found their resources to be quite respectable.

- **The Fussy Librarian** – Another low entry-point, promo site, this has services in the $10 - $57 range and is the third hist ranked on this list.

- **Robin Reads** – Ranging from $40 - $80 for services, this one seems to service the smaller independents. Of all the book promo sites that have been included in this list, it is the only one that does not have active Twitter/X marketing.

This is a selection of ten of "the best book promo sites." Your research may encounter numerous others. There could also be an entirely different list depending on the markets that you wish to sell to. There are undoubtedly many options, services, track records, and other variables to consider beyond mere price point.

For me, this list is remarkable valuable and I look forward to using it to extend and grow my abilities in **The Art of the Book Hustle**.

## Kindlepreneur's Book Launch Strategy
Created by Dave Chesson: "Real Authors Deserve to be Read!"

As you must take the time to properly introduce your newly completed book to the marketplace, it is important to *not overlook* the critical importance of a well-planned book launch strategy. Kindlepreneur has suggested that these following be utilized:

- **Launch Preparations**
  - While Writing
    - Build an ARC team
    - Contact editorial reviewers
    - Start building relationships with other authors
  - As Soon as Writing Complete
    - Send ARC copies out to ARC Team: Steps
    - Contact other authors and send ARC for editorial review
  - As Soon as Cover Created
    - Post on social media your cover reveal
    - Update your social media header image
    - Create inventory of promo images
- **Pre Launch Actions**
  - T-1 Month – Prepare which list of book promotion sites
    - T-1 Week – Contact authors who got an ARC to get reviews
    - Contact your ARC Team
    - Test your book description blurb
  - T-1 Day – Contact your ARC Team
- **Launch Day**

- Set price to 0.99
- Send personalized emails to ARC Team to leave reviews
  - Include a special review link to your Team
- Send email to ARC authors thanking them
  - Include special review link for authors
- Contact Amazon to switch to preferred categories
- Update previously published books' back matter with the new book's link
- **Prior to Marketing Efforts**
  - Create Amazon Ads to keep sales momentum going
  - Promote the launch via BookBub ads
- **Extra Marketing Tactics**
  - Stream Live on Facebook or YouTube
    - Q&A
    - Discuss motivation in writing or elements of writing
  - Post images of celebrating with your new book
- **Post Launch Strategy**
  - T+3
    - Change price to normal price (usually $2.99)
    - Check that Amazon put you in the right categories
    - Send email to your list announcing new book
    - Post on social media about your book's launch
  - T+5
    - Initiate a book promotion using one of the book promotion sites
    - Schedule another Author's email blast of your book
    - Send email to unopened on your email list
  - T+7
    - Initiate a book promotion using one of the book promotion sites
    - Send email to your email list
  - T+9

- Initiate a book promotion using one of the book promotion sites
- Send email with request for a review to your list
  o T+11
    - Initiate a book promotion using one of the book promotion sites

## Kindle Keyword Strategy for Nonfiction Authors

Everything in this chapter is taken directly from the Kindlepreneur web destination. For much of what I am sharing is directly quoted from KDP books. In a few instances, I have translated their ideas into my own words. Still, I own them all the credit for what I am sharing.

> While ⬚action keywords can be a little harder to pin down (it is possible, see here), nonfiction books have always been the area where keywords can really excel in helping you gain sales and increase your book ranking.

> You see, shoppers type what they are looking for into Amazon in the hopes that a solution to their problem will be in the results. The terms these people use should therefore become the basis of what you put into your book's title, subtitle, and your 7 Kindle Keywords.

You will be putting these keywords into your process for listing your book for sale on Amazon. The following suggestions are very important for your ultimate success. Please pay close attention to the following from Kindlepreneur:

> The first step in researching your keywords is to start with a brainstorming session. And with nonfiction, you probably have a good idea of some keywords to start with,

but there are four different categories that you should consider when brainstorming your ideas.

**Four Nonfiction Keyword Categories:**

- **Pain Points** – These "help you target the problems people have that motivate them to search for a book to help with those problems. People don't buy nonfiction just because they want to learn. They do so because something caused them to feel that they were lacking in some area and wanted to find a solution."

- **Desired Results** – To be considered "Second only to pain points in importance, the solution is going to be one of your biggest selling points. If you've got a problem, people aren't searching to know more about that problem. They are searching for something to fix that problem."

- **Emotional Amplifiers** – These words are employed because they "will create immediacy, specificity, or enhances the solutions talked above in the last section… It's good to come up with a solid list of emotional amplifiers that could apply to your problem and solution."

- **Demographics** – "If you intend to target a specific demographic with a solution geared toward them, you are much more likely to find success. For example, weight loss is a huge topic and you have almost no chance of ranking for that keyword. But weight loss for women over 60 is a completely different story. Now, your target market is considerably smaller, and now that you've niched down, you've got a much better chance of actually coming up in a search."

Finally, the article recommends that you take the time to "find the right combination of phrases" using keywords.

You've come up with a list of potential keywords and topics to research. However, one or two-word keywords is often going to be too broad. You want to take your list (in all four categories above) and start mixing and matching them until you find some that reach a good niche.

# Marketing Strategies Checklist

1. Make your book into a brand.

2. Make your book into an online course.

3. Create a well-crafted and stylish author website.

4. Create an email database that you will frequently update and grow.

5. Create a presence on popular social media sites.

6. Put together a blog post where you share excerpts and related writings.

7. Subscribe to a quality email distribution service.

8. Be sure to include a subscribe button to your website and blog postings.

9. Set up an audio or video podcast.

10. Create a Facebook business page for your book.

11. Regularly provide up-to-date, interesting content on your social media platforms.

12. Inquire about running ads on Facebook to promote your book.

13. Amazon also has paid ads to promote your products.

14. Carefully pick the correct audience for your book.

15. Build a database of book reviewers.

16. Offer your book for free on Amazon, such as Kindle ebooks.

17. Post frequently across Facebook, LinkedIn, Instagram, and other social media platforms.

18. Create a WhatsApp group for people who share your primary interests.

19. Look for multiple distributors to widen your marketing geography.

20. Engage in book signings and readings in popular local stores,

21. Link up with book promotion sites.

22. Hire a public relations agent to push you out to extensive media sources.

23. Set up a high-quality broadcast desk at your home or office; be sure to choose a high-quality camera with adequate Internet bandwidth and a classy-looking background.

24. Find opportunities to guest write for online news and information sites.

25. Offer limited-time discounts for purchasing your book.

26. Extend significant discounts for bulk purchases.

27. Access book discussion forums and study groups.

28. Consider launching a book study group in a popular local bookstore; don't ignore the smaller independent booksellers.

29. Engage in a series of web meetings to discuss critical issues for which your book serves cutting-edge strategies.

30. Put your book into writers' competitions.

31. Attend writers' conferences and book festivals; consider getting your booth or sharing booth space with one or more others.

32. Seek out and accept invitations to speak at conferences and events where large audiences can be introduced to your work.

33. Launch a YouTube channel or other online streaming media (I use YT, Facebook Live, Linked-In Live, and YouNow).

34. Employ the services of a marketing specialist.

35. Study and learn to apply Guerilla Marketing strategies practically.

36. Organize your author's website to maximize SEO (search engine optimization). It would be helpful to refer to the chapter on Kindlepreneur's "Trigger Words for Books."

37. Team up with popular online influencers.

38. Engage book giveaways to help to build your email database.

39. Build an interactive community with those who share the values and missions expressed in your writing.

40. Create "merch" or "swag" associated with your brand.

41. Share your merch with your best, most enthusiastic fans.

42. Print postcards, business cards, and other materials that you can distribute to promote your work.

43. Make sure that your book is priced correctly for the marketplace.

44. Review others' books to get your name associated with their fanbase.

45. Constantly study to upgrade your functional knowledge of marketing and sales.

46. Put together a brief, well-crafted electronic media kit with a professional photo, author bio, relevant contact information, and links to any media where you've been featured.

47. Periodically update your whole promotional package and keep your contact information current.

48. Acquire an online payments system.

49. Build your independent store online to market your books and related merchandise.

50. Create interactive processes that engage you with readers, who you intend to turn into superfans.

51. Create a "lead magnet," which builds your database by giving something away to those interested.

52. Collaborate with other authors and cross-promote.

53. Never miss the opportunity to remind your audience that you have an informative book for sale.

54. Set up a text message service for people to express their interest in expanding contact with you.

55. Build an avatar or "proto-persona" representing your ideal audience member and target market.

56. Create an avatar of your ideal reader and identify geographical locations where your ideal readers are found.

57. Select a few local or regional libraries where your book can be added to their catalogs. You would prefer to sell copies to a city-wide or regional library network; if needed, donate copies, although most libraries are set up to purchase books.

58. Get your books into the hands of professors and other education professionals.

59. Identify niche categories to serve as keywords that overlap with the central themes included in your writing.

60. Put together a powerful list of keywords that are embedded in your body of work that the book represents.

61. Identify social activist groups or non-governmental organizations (NGOs) whose missions synchronize with your book themes. Consider donating a few copies or offering them at a significant discount.

62. Include social media hashtags linking your book to issues of high interest.

63. Ensure that your book description is optimized for marketing on Amazon, Barnes & Noble, and other online sellers; it should likely be highly reflective of your back cover text.

64. Push sample chapters of your book across social media for others to peruse.

65. If your book sales go cold or never really sparked, consider redoing the book cover using a professional graphic artist.

66. Continue to practice and perfect the five-word, seven-word, and fifteen-word strategies, along with the thirty-second elevator pitch to quickly spark interest in your body of work.

67. Be generous, giving, and empathetic in all your encounters; there is a natural tendency of reciprocity for people to give back to sharing and caring people.

68. As you are critical of societal trends that negatively impact people's lives, be cautious about criticizing vulnerable groups for having bought into depraved and degenerate patterns; you always want to come off as genuinely caring and helpful.

69. Craft a vocal style that always sounds highly professional when you are invited to speak in public or via all communications; go into a character that speaks as informed and authentic.

70. Consider setting up a Goodreads page for your work.

71. Assemble a collection of testimonials from those who have benefited from your work or who have reviewed it and have a large following that values their opinion.

72. Team up with others whose outreach overlaps with yours and create programs and seminars where your mutual interests consolidate an expanded curriculum.

73. Set up pre-orders of your book with early-bird discounts to maximize your book launch.

74. Schedule a formal book launch event with several months' advance notice.

75. Sign up for affiliate programs for online sellers like Amazon.

76. Assemble a "street team" of enthusiasts of your work and reward them for generating interest, gathering emails, and increasing book sales.

77. Create a short book trailer with a crisp video that has been professionally edited.

78. Bundle your books, or collaborate with other authors, to offer a bigger value to the buyers.

79. Create multi-tiered marketing and promotional strategies.

80. Periodically engage email analytics to track your email openings, video viewings, and other means of comparing which marketing strategies have yielded the greatest ROI.

81. Identify and compare the various book marketing resources that exist.

82. Craft a superbly written press release; keep it current with periodic updating and rewriting.

83. Plan a speaking tour.

84. Engage in an online blogging tour utilizing complimentary sites.

85. Don't overlook local television and radio, which may be proud to feature a local author.

86. Always keep your mind focused, aware, and open to new ways to market successfully to your audience; never stop being a creative author/bookseller!

87. Write a professional and interesting author bio. Keep it brief; do not use it as an autobiography.

88. Make your book available to purchase at your online store.

89. Come up with ideas for merchandise related to your book(s).

90. Host contests where your fans can submit entries for merchandise designs.

91. Have pages on your author's website for book reviews, FAQs, and testimonials.

92. Make a 'Discussion' page on your website specifically for questions, comments, visitor-posted ideas, and promotional strategies authors have employed.

93. Help aspiring authors do what you do. Write an advice column on your website for aspiring authors.

94. Get to the point. Add buttons to your web postings and site that take viewers straight to your social media sites.

95. Keep your website clean and easy to navigate (like they do at SmithPublicity.com). Too many bells and whistles are distracting; simpler is almost always better.

96. Generate online ideas to market your book for free. A lot of places online don't cost anything, but can help you sell more books and related merchandise.

97. Become widely accessible across online media. Through maximizing your online footprint and growing virtual platforms, you make yourself visible in a crowded space.

98. Have a virtual book tour and plan a broad-based cost-effective online campaign.

99. Create weekly or monthly newsletters and ask fans to sign onto your email list to access them.

100. Google's pay-per-click advertising might be something to consider to see if it is appropriate for your publication.

101. Submit your website to related groups, companies, or organizations that have a website directory.

102. Search out and build collaboration by sharing valuable resources with site owners that would find those resources to be worth sharing.

103. Research your competitors to ascertain the roots of their successes that you might yet have achieved.

104. Blogging will help your website SEO and organic traffic and serve as a means to get the word out about you as an author and the books that you have written. Post regularly to a blog that is easily found via your website. This is how an author can stay connected and active online. Blogs are an ideal way to share your knowledge with others.

105. Respond to commentary and questions on your blog promptly, and welcome new and creative ideas offered in the comments.

106. Offer to be a guest blogger on other popular blogs as a published author promoting one's book. This can be particularly effective on special interest blogs.

107. Reciprocate with other bloggers that support your book promotion efforts.

108. Create an RSS Feed and place it on Feedburner.com. This will allow you to gather insights about your readers.

109. Go eBook – As many more people are using electronic book readers, converting your hardcover or paperback book into an eBook will increase book sales.

110. Running an eBook promo will attract more attention to your book. Offer people an incentive to buy and read your eBook. It will increase your book's exposure, and the number of reviews, recommendations, and sales.

111. Use BookBub to create a profile for your eBook promo.

112. Author-centered discussion forums allow authors to connect and talk about marketing strategies and how to increase sales.

113. Make the time for data analytics. Crunching numbers might not be as fun as writing, but it helps to prevent wasting money on campaigns that don't work effectively.

114. Continue publishing new books. Nothing sells backlist like frontlist! Continually publishing new books will help you garner a wider audience that will be interested in your previous books.

115. Forums are often an important place to connect with fellow authors, others in your industry, and potential readers. There are many forums to be found online. Join several and remain active in participating and helping to promote the forums.

116. Create/join a forum (it doesn't have to be specifically related to books or publishing) and actively participate in its community.

117. Using social media to help market a book. Author publicity by a book marketing 101 for independent and self-published authors.

118. How to use Facebook to promote book sales, get more book reviews, and spark visibility for your novel, cookbook or historical nonfiction manuscript.

119. Although several new social media groups have become popular, Facebook is still relevant and remains important for promoting authors. Having a Facebook page for your author brand is critical because it lends legitimacy to your book, yourself as a professional and also serves as another means to promote your book and everything that comes along with it. These would include events, give-aways, future projects, and and online forums. It's important to portray your authentic self on FaceBook. Stay true to *you* and build a large supportive community.

120. Create a Facebook page geared toward you as a professional author – not your personal life.

121. Give fans the option to post their book reviews, testimonials, comments, and questions to your Facebook page.

122. Learn how to use Twitter hashtags to help with increasing your book sales and reach your audience.

123. If you have the time to do it right, Twitter can be your most powerful social media tool. Hashtags, particularly, reign supreme on Twitter and are a great way to find potential readers and others to network with, and also to be found. As with other social media platforms, Twitter helps you connect with your community and lends legitimacy to your brand.

124. Create a Twitter account to tweet updates about new books, book tours, book trailers, media coverage of you and your book, etc. For example, here's our Twitter page.

125. Provide fans with a hashtag for promoting your new book.

126. Use Twitter hashtags for events, news, promotions, etc.

127. 101 Marketing Tips that will help you sell more books! – Click to tweet.

128. These marketing strategies from @SmithPublicity really helped me as a new author. – Click to tweet.

129. LinkedIn is a great place to network with other writers and authors. LinkedIn is the largest professional networking tool in the world.

130. Create a LinkedIn author page to connect to community.

131. LinkedIn is the largest professional networking tool in the world. You can use LinkedIn to attend offline events, write articles, join groups, post videos and photos, and more.

132. Create a LinkedIn page to connect to other authors and professionals in the writing world and related industries. LinkedIn has increasingly become the most popular professional networking platform. Remember that LinkedIn is searchable, so incorporate keywords people might search for on your main page. And post regularly, more is better, but once a week is fine. View our LinkedIn page here.

133. Create your YouTube account to help market your book. YouTube is a great place for authors to promote their books for free. Make sure to create a playlist of your videos so that the YouTube algorithm can find them.

134. YouTube is one of the most powerful search engines on the Internet, and it's incredibly easy to create video content. Like your website, your videos don't need to be slickly produced; today, most smartphones can produce nice looking videos that will work fine. As a general rule, keep your videos short – no more than a few minutes. Obviously,

if you're posting a video of a book event you had or a speech you gave, these much longer videos are fine. Like other platforms, YouTube is keyword driven, so make sure you use the video description section to incorporate keywords that people may use to find an author or book like yours.

135. Describe your channel and videos. Also create playlists of your videos so that the algorithm can understand it better.

136. Link your YouTube videos on your Facebook and Twitter accounts.

137. Compile a series of short videos of you discussing topics related to your book. Make them informational, not promotional, and employ them in all marketing services and activities.

138. Amazon is the world's largest online bookseller. Selling your book on Amazon is essential. We have some strategies and tips to optimize your Amazon channel.

139. Love it or hate it, every author needs Amazon! Some authors dislike the way Amazon can discount prices, but remember, people want to buy books from sources they trust. You may not make as much from each book sale on Amazon as compared to directly selling them from your website, but you'll end up making more money because more people will buy from Amazon, and few will likely buy from your website.

140. Go to Amazon and register as an author. Be sure to create a compelling and robust author central page.

141. When selling your books on Amazon, follow the wealth of information and advice Amazon offers and incorporate ideas into your plan.

142. Try to get fans to post their book reviews and testimonials on Amazon.

143. Join Amazon's affiliate program.

144. Old-fashioned networking still works and is the best way to promote sales. – Networking, whether the old-fashioned meet and greets or the cyber type, the principle remains the same – make authentic connections with people – the type of people you want to know about you! Networking can lead to a wide variety of opportunities, beyond just spreading word about your book.

145. Attend book publishing events and writers' conferences and distribute information about your book, business cards, etc.

146. Offer to speak to your local chamber of commerce about a topic related to your book.

147. Check for local meet-up groups that relate to your book topic.

148. Go to local and regional general networking groups – most areas have professional networking events for a wide variety of businesses, interests, hobbies, etc.

149. Check for local activity clubs. You might be surprised how many there are, and these can be great places to potentially offer to speak to the group on a topic related to your group.

150. Any author can join Goodreads' Author Program for free. As long as you have a published book or have a manuscript that will be published soon, you can create an Author page on Goodreads for free book publicity. Goodreads boasts the world's largest community of book lovers – so of course, you'll want to be a part of it! Users of Goodreads can generate reading lists, review books, keep track of the books they've read, and more. By having your book available on Goodreads, you will reach a larger audience of book lovers. Think of Goodreads as the virtual "word of mouth" for

books; if one user reads and recommends your book, word can spread like wildfire. Go to Goodreads and register as an author.

151. Develop all of your profile pages by adding a photo and bio.

152. Add the Goodreads Author widget to your website.

153. Offline marketing tips for authors of newly published books. These can include going on a book tour, having a book launch or speaking at a local bookstore.

154. The Internet is everywhere and affects everything, but believe it or not, there is life outside of the Web! In person connections and conversations are still high valued, and there are many ways you can make the most of face-to-face time and other marketing collateral in the "real world." Just as there's no replacement for turning the pages of a physical book, offline marketing opportunities are not to be underestimated.

155. Organize a team for your book launch.

156. Contact a local bookstore or other venues about hosting a book release party.

157. Design merchandise for your books and consider a targeted advertisement.

158. Make business cards with your photo and addresses to your author's website and social media profile pages.

159. Speak to book clubs about writing in your genre – book genre marketing can be a surprisingly effective addition to your promotional campaign.

160. Have book readings for your new book. Some possible venues: Retirement homes, Elementary, junior high, or high schools depending on your target age group, Coffee shops,

Community colleges, nearby universities, locally owned bookstores, rehab centers, hospitals, libraries, Google+ Hangout, churches, the setting (town, city) of your book, community events (i.e. fairs, picnics, festivals).

161. Have book signings for your new book.

162. Contact your local paper and ask them if they'd be interested in interviewing you. Contact the local paper of the town your book is set in about interviewing you.

163. Contact your local radio station and ask them if they'd be interested in having you on their show. (These radio interview tips can help if you get on the air.) Contact the local radio station of the town your book is set in about having you on their show.

164. Create an affiliate program in addition to joining existing affiliate programs.

165. Partner with organizations, clubs, and other groups that support a cause similar to the one that your book addresses.

166. Hire a company to help reach the market for your finished book. An author's fans are their greatest asset in the marketplace. Author publicity companies prepare you for speaking events on Tedx, book launches with a dedicated book launch team, and book signings.

167. Fans can be your evangelists ... spreading the word about your book far and wide! You want to create authentic relationships and cater to your fanbase, because they are the most important asset you have.

168. Offer your devoted fans sneak previews of your new book.

169. Offer your devoted fans advance copies of your new book.

170. Have a page on your website for short stories, and add a new one every week or month, depending on your schedule.

171. Promote each weekly short story on Facebook and Twitter.

172. Host a contest for topic suggestions for your weekly short story.

173. Host a contest for the best short story where the winner will have their story featured on your website.

174. Link to the winner's story on your social media pages.

175. Have free book giveaway contests for your fans and website visitors.

176. Celebrate your fans by featuring a Fan of the Month on your website and social media profiles.

177. Host a contest for the best illustration of a scene from one of your books where the winner will have his/her illustration featured on your website.

178. Link to the winner's illustration on your social media pages.

179. Host a contest for the best book trailer where the winner will have his/her trailer featured on your website.

180. Link to the winner's book trailer on your social media pages.

181. Host a contest where your fans can submit a movie of them acting their favorite scene in one of your books and feature the winner on your website.

182. Link to the winner's movie on your social media pages.

183. Host a costume contest around Halloween for the best costume of one of your major characters where the winner will be featured on your website.

184. Link to the winner's picture of him/her in the costume on your social profiles.

185. Create fan pages for the main characters in your book.

186. Ask fans to post pictures of them reading your book.

187. Get to know your fans even better by polling them on their likes, dislikes, and opinions on your ideas for books or promotions.

188. Write a book specifically for your fans.

189. Write a book that your fans can customize by picking what happens next.

190. Going the extra mile to promote your indie book could mean researching other nonfiction book titles for compatible audiences, hiring a video company to make a book trailer, or renting book advertising space on a low-cost billboard in your home city.

191. Go the Extra Mile. Marketing a book is more a marathon than a sprint; it takes time, persistent effort, and dedication. Even if you hire a professional book publicist, you must still be involved and help promote your activities. Sustained, well-planned, and diverse book promotion will almost always lead to positive things.

192. Make a book trailer, or hire a professional to make one.

193. Offer to write articles for a magazine related to your genre.

194. Host a seminar or webinar for aspiring writers.

195. Advertise on a low-cost billboard.

196. Become a featured content writer for some websites related to your genre, being an author, writing your first book, etc.

197. Donate your books to places where your target audience is located: elementary, junior high, or high schools, daycare centers, and libraries.

198. Link up with libraries in the town where your book is set, along with camps, community centers, YMCAs, senior centers, retirement communities, homeless shelters, and prisons.

199. Seek connections to local colleges or colleges in the town where your book is set.

200. Utilize publicity services like Help A Reporter Out (HARO)

201. Author podcasts are growing in popularity and are a great way to get free marketing for your book. Host a discussion on a related topic and invite guests to speak on your podcast. In turn, become a guest on other podcasts to find opportunities to market a book for free.

202. Podcasts are booming in popularity! They represent a great opportunity for authors because they allow for long-form, uninterrupted interviews, and casual conversation. They are also becoming a popular tool for authors who create their own podcasts.

203. Do some basic Google searches to find podcasts that pertain to your book, then reach out and offer yourself as a guest. Remember that popular podcasts book guests months in advance, so contact them early.

204. Listen to educational podcasts that will help you learn about books and marketing, such as "All Things Book Marketing."

205. Check out authors in your genre who have podcasts.

206. Start your own podcast! It's not as hard as you think. Invest in some low-cost editing software for podcasts, such as Wavepad.

207. Some tricks of the trade that only the best book marketers-for-hire know about. We have insider knowledge and experience with what works and what doesn't. Don't hire a

book marketer on Fivrr without checking to see if they have any experience first.

208. As professional book publicists, the experts at Smith Publicity have developed many creative ways to get attention for a book. Remember to think outside the box and expand your comfort level.

209. Send your book to a producer or editor via Fed Ex or UPS – it is much more likely to be opened.

210. If you're pitching to be on a radio or TV show and your book is fiction, lead with why you'd be a great interview, and don't announce that you've written a novel. Broadcast outlets are more inclined to interview nonfiction authors, so make them love your pitch and not focus on the kind of book you've written.

211. When sending a book to a media contact, print or write "requested material" on the envelope.

212. Leave a copy of your book on a train or bus, and put a sticker on it that says, "Free book, please pass along when done." Now, that is thinking outside the box.

213. Listen to talk radio, watch TV interview shows, read magazines and newspapers, review online news sites … and see how other authors are being featured!

214. Optimize a book for effective promotional accessibility.

215. Survey your target audience. Ask questions about demographics, psychographics, and online behavior to understand better where to market to readers and what messaging they'll respond to. Survey your existing audience and fans of comparable authors and books.

216. Conduct reader interviews. Learn how your readers find new books and make purchasing decisions. This will add

qualitative color to help you understand the quantitative survey data you analyze in spreadsheets.

217. Write reader personas. Write a short paragraph that describes each core group of readers you're targeting. Refer back to it whenever you're creating an ad, designing a cover, writing a tweet, or want a refresh on your audience's motives.

218. Create a list of targeting, and emotion-triggering keywords. Compile a list of search queries your target audience uses to search for books. Use tools like Google Trends and Google AdWords' Keyword tool to see which relevant queries are frequently used.

219. Create a plan to reach a targeted audience. Utilize this book's list of platforms and marketing tools to reach a specific target audience. For example, BookBub has 42 categories and millions of power readers, whom you can target with BookBub Ads or Featured Deals. There are also plenty of genre-specific blogs and publications you could target for promotions.

220. Take care to craft the perfect author website. Your site should be a marketing tool that serves as the hub of all your online activity, from blogging, selling books, emailing a newsletter, and participating in social media. Use a platform like WordPress, Squarespace, or Wix to build a site easily.

221. Set up a blog on your site. Provide readers with a "behind-the-scenes look" by blogging once or twice a month. Fans will love the insight into your personality and writing process, and anything you post is fodder for your next email to subscribers.

222. Link to your published books. Create a site page linking to your books to make it easy for readers to discover all the titles you've written. Include cover images, brief elevator pitches, and links to multiple retailers so readers can purchase your books wherever they shop.

223. Build a mailing list on your site. Include a simple form on your homepage, website pages, or blog's sidebar asking for visitors' email addresses. Collecting email addresses lets you build relationships with people who want to hear from you.

224. Welcome subscribers with an email autoresponse. When people subscribe to updates from you via your website, send them a welcome email, including either a link to a free ebook, sample chapters, or some manner of freebie as a "thank you" for signing up.

225. Claim your BookBub Author Profile. Make sure your BookBub Author Profile and all other online bios are up to date so fans and potential readers can learn more about what is ongoing about you and your books.

226. Get more BookBub followers. The more followers you have, the more people will receive dedicated emails from BookBub notifying them about your new releases and price promotions. And once you get 1K followers, you can also send BookBub Preorder Alerts!

227. Add a BookBub follow button to your site. Ensure that website visitors can find your BookBub Author Profile by adding a follow button or icon to your site, wherever it fits best into the site design.

228. Claim the broadest range of social media profiles that your *team* can maintain. Grab your username on Facebook, Twitter, Instagram, Pinterest, Tumblr, Google+, LinkedIn,

and About.me. Even if you don't have active profiles on each site, at least claim your name and direct people to visit your most active social media profiles instead.

229. Link to your website and BookBub Author Profile. Once you've created a website and claimed your BookBub Author Profile, make sure that people can find these assets by linking to them on your email signature and bio sections on your social media profiles.

230. Create multiple video blogs. Upload videos to YouTube or Vimeo, and embed each new video in a blog post. In these videos, you can answer fan questions, partner with another author to interview each other, list book recommendations, or do a short reading from an upcoming new release.

231. Experiment with a few simple videos to see if you're comfortable vlogging before focusing on production quality.

232. Toward designing your book's cover, if you are not adept at graphic art, then hire a cover designer. A great cover design can have a major impact on your sales numbers. For example, romance writer R.L. Mathewson went from selling five or six copies per day of her novel, Playing for Keeps, to over 1,000 per day by updating her cover design. It's usually worth it to hire a professional to create a polished cover that appeals to readers in your genre.

233. Test cover variations with your audience. Have your cover designer create multiple variations and use data to choose your cover design. Test two variations against each other using tools like PickFu, UsabilityHub, or Playbuzz.

234. Unify cover designs in a series. Create consistent branding between books in a series to make purchasing decisions easy for readers. A unified cover and title style often helps

readers recognize connected titles and encourages them to purchase subsequent books.

235. One tactic that has worked for me is to re-launch an older book with a new cover. Redesigning a book cover can be a great way to invigorate book sales. It gives you the opportunity to "re-launch" the book with updates and according to the ever-evolving tastes of genre readers.

236. Add a blurb to the cover. If you've managed to secure a blurb from a well-known author, consider including it on the book cover design. Try to use a short blurb so it's easy to read and you don't clutter the design.

237. Make book samples end on a cliffhanger. For example, on Amazon, users can download the first 10% of a book for free or read it on-site via the "Look Inside" feature. This gives you the opportunity to score a sale if the reader wants to continue after the sample.

238. Cross-promote books in the back matter. Include a list of all your titles in each of your books' back matter (not always easy to do when you have as many books as me). Update this back matter whenever you launch a new release. If you have the time, create a version of each book for each retailer with retailer-specific links to each book.

239. Include an excerpt in the back matter. Authors who include an excerpt see the highest increase in sales of their promoted book. Immediately after the acknowledgements, include the first chapter of the book you're promoting. Bookend the excerpt with links to purchase that book.

240. Link to your mailing list in the back matter. On your "About the Author" page, encourage readers to sign up for your mailing list. If they sign up, you'll be able to contact them

any time you want to promote your backlist titles, new releases, give-aways, price promotions, etc.

241. Optimize your book description. BookBub's A/B testing shows that descriptions that include quotes from authors, awards, and language that caters to your audience (e.g. "If you love thrillers, don't miss this action-packed read!") have higher engagement rates.

242. Include target keywords on product pages. Narrow down a list of 5-7 keywords your audience typically searches for, then incorporate these words into the description headline, description copy, and keyword sections on each retailer product page.

243. Choose relevant subcategories on retailer sites. This can increase your chances of being on the retailer bestseller charts for a specific category, which could drive higher sales volume. You'll also avoid disappointing readers who were expecting something different.

244. Tie different versions of a book together. Different authors and platforms use different systems, but find a way to connect a print edition with the ebook, audiobook, and international editions. This ensures that visitors to the product page can easily purchase the format they prefer.

245. Link series books by name. If you've published a book series, create a master name for the series and add it to the product's title on retailer sites. This will help retailer sites make automated recommendations within the series, and help readers find more books in the series to read.

246. Make books available globally. With growing book sales and millions of readers, international markets can be attractive targets for authors and publishers looking to expand their

potential readership. Optimize the cover design for each region and reach out to relevant local bloggers who can help spread the word.

247. Prepare an extensive list of your book marketing assets. (This extensive list is an example of such book marketing strategies and tactics, which, when acted upon, become assets.)

248. Write the ultimate elevator pitch. Write a concise, snappy pitch that shows what the book is about, what kind of world readers will be immersed in, why readers should care, and what accolades the book and author have received. A strong elevator pitch will make a book more enticing to readers deciding whether or not to purchase.

249. Test copy variations by polling readers. Use polling software like PickFu to test variations of description or marketing copy and see which your audience likes better. Always test and optimize to discover what copy will resonate best with readers.

250. A/B test marketing copy. Unlike polling, A/B tests give you quantitative data (i.e., the number of clicks). Use your email service provider to run A/B test emails and see which copy has the highest click-through rate, or use ad platforms like BookBub Ads and Facebook to A/B test your copy.

251. Get blurbs from reputable authors in your genre. Blurbs can catch readers' attention, especially if they're familiar with the quoting author or publication. Our tests showed that book descriptions including blurbs got an average of 22.6% higher click-through rates than those without blurbs.

252. Create images for teasers and quotes. You can easily turn book quotes into vibrant images using free apps like Canva

or Designfeed. Publish these teasers to your website and social media accounts in the weeks and months prior to a book's release.

253. We can't overstress the importance of runing a preorder campaign. Driving preorder sales can help a book hit various bestseller lists, since many retailers count all preorders as launch day sales. They also help build buzz and momentum for a new book, leading to word-of-mouth sales later.

254. Tease your audience with a title reveal. Create buzz for an upcoming book by announcing the title. Some authors get creative by posting a video announcing a book's title. Post a cover reveal on a popular blog. Partner with a blog or website that's popular amongst readers in your genre to host a reveal. If you can arrange to have a book available for preorder in time for its reveal. Link to a page where readers can preorder as a great way to jump-start preorder sales.

255. Link to a preorder in previous books' back matter. This lets readers order it as soon as they finish the previous book, without having to remember to buy the new book when it's available for download. Include an excerpt of the upcoming book in the back matter, even if it's unedited, to provide a sneak-peek.

256. Send a BookBub Preorder Alert. A Preorder Alert is a dedicated email to an author's BookBub followers announcing that one of the author's books is available for preorder. They're highly targeted since they're only sent to an author's followers, and at only $0.02 per eligible follower, they're a cost effective way to promote a preorder. BookBub ads let advertisers market any book at any time to BookBub's millions of power readers — including preorders, new releases, and full-priced books!

257. Offer gifts in exchange for preorders. This provides an extra incentive since they can't get the instant gratification of reading the book right away. Have readers email a screenshot or picture of their receipt to receive the gift.

258. Consider sending a digital gift pack to readers who preorder. Sending swag via mail can get expensive, so digital gifts can be more convenient. This could include exclusive content like short stories, author commentary, deleted scenes, or high-rez posters.

259. You can use tools like NetGalley or Edelweiss to find early reviewers reviews before the book launches, or reach out to relevant bloggers with a pitch on the book. They can't review books on retailer sites until release day, but can post the reviews to their websites, blogs, or Goodreads.

260. Offer free eBooks to Amazon top reviewers. Reach out to Amazon users with a "Top Reviewer" badge who've reviewed books similar to yours. They will likely have a quick turnaround on reading and reviewing.

261. Book give-aways can take various forms, including blog tours, contests on your blog or Facebook page. Offering copies to your most loyal fans in exchange for an honest review can help with traction as it rewards them for their loyalty.

262. Ask readers to review a book in the back matter. A high number of reviews makes a book more enticing to potential readers. When a book has at least 150 five-star reviews on Amazon or Goodreads, including that number of five-star reviews in the copy increased clicks an average of 14.1%.

263. Submit a book for relevant editorial reviews. Many genres have publications like RT Book Reviews where authors can

submit their books for editorial reviews. Some of these publications require submitting your book months before publication, so plan early!

264. Add each book to your BookBub Author Profile as soon as the preorder page or product page is live on retailer sites. This will ensure that your BookBub followers receive a New Release Alert when each book launches.

265. Brand your homepage with a new release. Publicize your latest book on your website by updating the header or banners of your homepage to increase awareness among website visitors. Consider including blurbs instead of a synopsis to intrigue visitors.

266. Link to your newest release. Find a high-visibility place to link to your book. Many authors choose to include links in their personal email signature, Twitter bio, Facebook page bio, About.me page, and LinkedIn bio. Update these assets whenever you release a new book.

267. Add a free ebook sampler to retailer sites. Upload the sampler as its own ebook with a separate product page and make it clear in the title and description that this is just a sample — the first chapter or first few chapters — to avoid disappointing readers. On the last page, include a link to purchase the full copy.

268. Upload a PDF sample to your website. Once people download it, it's okay if the PDF is distributed outside of your control since it's just a sample. In fact, you should hope it gets as many eyeballs on it as possible! On the last page, include a link to purchase the full copy.

269. Add an excerpt to Wattpad, a social network for authors and readers with tens of millions of users. Writers can share

their stories for free, and readers can vote on them and leave feedback. Bestselling authors share excerpts of their books on Wattpad and link to the retailer pages where readers can purchase the full book to find out what happens next.

270. Swag can be an effective marketing tool, especially if it ties into the story in some way. Remember: everyone gives away bookmarks and bookplates. Consider your target audience, and think about what they would have a real use for that relates to the book.

271. Sell themed merchandise on your website. Create custom t-shirts, coffee mugs, ereader covers, jewelry, framed art, etc., and have them available for sale on your website or at events. Services like CafePress can help.

272. Submit a book as an award contender. Including an author's awards in BookBub's blurbs increases clicks an average of 6.7%. Find relevant or genre-specific awards and submit a book for consideration.

273. Temporarily discount a backlist book to drive sales. Choose as low a price as possible to drive the highest volume of sales. 95% of bargain readers have purchased a book from an author unknown to them because of a price promotion.

274. Promote a full-priced book in a discounted book's back matter. Authors see a 2.2x higher increase in sales of other books in their series if links are included in the back matter of the discounted book.

275. Discount the first book in a series. Hook new readers into a series by pricing low. 77% of bargain readers buy full-priced ebooks, so getting them hooked on a series via a discount often leads to full-priced sales later.

276. Create a permafree gateway book. For example, the first book in a series can be permafree as a gateway to the rest of the series — BookBub readers are 10x more likely to click on a book that's offered for free than a discounted book.

277. Run price promotions in foreign countries. Discounting a book in foreign markets can be a great way to drive ebook downloads and revenue in those regions. Also, when you submit a book for a BookBub Featured Deal, you can easily elect to run the promotion in our international editions.

278. Run a price promo when you launch a new book. If you're promoting a new release, running a price promotion for a backlist book can help drive sales for the new book. 89% of BookBub partners who discounted an older book to market a new release sold more of their new book after the promotion. Or try discounting the new book once it's built up a solid platform!

279. Email your mailing list about a book launch. Reach out to fans who have opted in to receive communication from you. You can also reach out to them and let them know about an imminent release. Use an exclusive look at the first chapter to get them excited.

280. Later, email the recipients who clicked. The people who opened or clicked on the book launch email are the most engaged people on your list. They will be most likely to make the purchase or even write a review of the book. Reach out and ask if they've read it yet. Let them know you value their opinion and would sincerely appreciate an honest review.

281. Later, email those who didn't click. Don't forget the people who didn't engage with the book launch email — they cared enough to specifically sign up for your email list, but for whatever reason didn't open the first email. Send them the

first few chapters of the book for free and see if you can hook them a second time around.

282. Promote a book on relevant blogs. Compile a list of book bloggers and reviewers who regularly review books, interview authors, or feature guest posts from authors in your genre. Coordinate with them to promote giveaways or publish reviews or author interviews.

283. Sign up as a HARO source. Help a Reporter Out (HARO) connects journalists with relevant experts, and you are the expert of your niche! Sign up and you'll receive an email three times per day that includes opportunities in which you could be quoted. Reply quickly for the best chance of getting selected for a quote in an article. Ask for a link back to your site.

284. Partner with other authors to run themed promotions. For example, if your publishing imprint or group of friends has three fantasy books featuring fae, coordinate price promotions, themed blog posts, and social media parties. Packaging these books promotionally helps each book gain exposure across the other authors' platforms.

285. Create a relevant video series. Create mini documentaries on a book, or get more creative. For example, for a chick lit book featuring a hairdresser protagonist, create a cute series of hair tutorials featuring hairstyles from the book. For a middle grade mystery featuring a magician, create a magic trick tutorial series. Publish the videos on YouTube and your other social channels.

286. Run a Google AdWords campaign. Target keywords that your audience would likely search for to find books similar to yours. Create several versions of ad copy within each ad

group and let Google automatically run each variation and determine a winner.

287. Time book promotions with current events and during specific seasons, an annual event, or when something pops in the media, take advantage of that opportunity and be a part of the conversation.

288. Write and syndicate a press release. Create an informational press release announcing the new book. Link to both the new release product page and your own website for SEO purposes. You can take advantage of a free press release distribution service to syndicate the press release to news websites and blogs.

289. Reach out to the press. Email relevant media sites a pitch for a book and offer a free copy. Be sure to use a catchy subject line and opening sentence. Follow up by sending a press release and personalized letter with the book.

290. Participate in relevant interviews. Agree to participate in interviews that would effectively reach your target audience. Interviews can be a great way to share your perspectives without needing to write much original content.

291. Submit a post to Buzzfeed. Write a clever or funny tie-in to a book. The article you write can either be entirely about the book, a "which character are you" quiz, or an indirectly related listicle. For example, a romance author can write a post on "10 Sizzling Beaches Where You Can Read Steamy Romances" and incorporate her book into the post.

292. Sites like Facebook and Twitter let you target ads to a fine-tuned audience based on preferences users have expressed

on those platforms. This enables you to advertise the book to people interested in similar books or genres.

293. An author's social media images — such as on Facebook and Twitter — offer a great branding opportunity for authors. Update your cover photo with branding for your latest release, preorder, or price promotion to ensure everyone on the page knows about it.

294. Make your blog posts easy to share. Make it easy for fans to share your book news and other blog posts by optimizing each post for social sharing. Tools like AddThis or ShareThis add social sharing buttons alongside each post and ClickToTweet to create clickable tweets.

295. Make each social media post visual. Tweets with images get 150% more retweets, and Facebook posts with images account for 87% of total interactions. Include an image of the book's cover or a teaser quote. This can encourage fans to click, share, or like. Check out Canva, Shutterstock, and iStock for usable images.

296. Run a fan art contest. Get fans to upload fan art of a character or scene from a book on your blog or Facebook page — or have them share it using a hashtag on Instagram or Twitter. Choose a winner to receive a prize (and then get permission to use that fan art in your marketing).

297. Ask questions and encourage participation from your extended creative community. The more your fans and followers engage with your updates, the more exposure you'll get — so make sure to involve fans in a two-way conversation.

298. Pre-schedule social media content. Doing social media marketing doesn't mean spending all day online. Use tools

like Buffer, TweetDeck, or Hootsuite to schedule your day's or week's social media content in advance. This will free up your time for writing and other marketing efforts.

299. Pin important updates on your feed. You can pin important announcements about new releases, sales, or contests to the top of your Facebook page and Twitter profile. You only need to post the content once. Then, you can pin it for higher visibility!

300. Host a release party on Facebook. Run a contest on launch day, giving people many opportunities to win prizes, such as a free book copy, gift cards, posters, and more.

301. Post behind-the-scenes looks on Instagram of your workspace, character sketches you drew, index cards laid out for plotting, or something to show your personality and a peek into your mind when writing.

302. Create Pinterest boards of inspiration showing off your workspace wish list, what inspired you when writing, or fan art for your books.

303. Run a trivia contest on Tumblr. Readers love a fun challenge!

304. Host author Q&As on Zoom or stream a Facebook Live video Q&A. When you begin a Facebook Live video, people who've liked your page are notified that you're streaming live. Afterward, the video is available for anyone to watch on your Facebook page, and they'll see the comments come in as though they're watching live!

305. Host a Q&A session on Twitter. Create a hashtag for the Q&A session — it can be a one-time occasion or a monthly event. Promote the Q&A beforehand so your fans know to either block the time in their calendar or schedule their tweets to post during the Q&A.

306. Host a Reddit "Ask Me Anything" (AMA). Many authors host AMAs on Reddit, answering reader questions throughout a set time. Submit an AMA to the IAmA group or peruse Reddit for genre-specific subreddits to find opportunities to host an AMA.

307. Answer relevant questions on Quora. If you've published a nonfiction book or have become a subject-matter expert via research you've done for a fiction book, follow relevant topics on Quora and answer questions as you see fit. Include the link to the book in your Quora bio.

308. Host a Q&A via Snapchat and YouTube. Have fans send questions directly to your Snapchat account and answer them later via a live or pre-recorded video on your YouTube channel. For tech-savvy authors, this twist on the traditional Q&A is an innovative way to keep readers engaged.

309. Create reader communities by building an author street team. A street team is a group of fans volunteering to promote an author. The goal of a street team is to incite word-of-mouth buzz for a book, and they're motivated by their love of the author's work. Some authors use Facebook groups to organize their street teams and recruit new members.

310. Create an author fan club. Fan clubs are groups where readers can congregate without the expectation of helping with promotional activities. Fans can interact with the author, discuss books, and have other fun conversations with like-minded readers.

311. Host a read-along group. Create a virtual book club where participants read a designated number of chapters of a book per week and discuss them in the group. Having the author

participate in the group greatly incentivizes fans to join the conversation.

312. Launch a Facebook group with other authors. For example, The Jewels of Historical Romance has a Facebook group of over 2K members that 12 romance authors created. They cross-promote each other's books, hold monthly joint giveaways and contests, and announce new releases. It's a free and creative way for each author to expand their fan base.

313. Create box sets and bundles of the first few books in a series. Include the first two or three books of a series in a box set to promote a full-price book later in the series. This can be a great way to hook readers and make them invested in the characters so they're willing to pay full price to know how the tale ends. Promote the next book in the series in the box set's back matter.

314. Create a box set for standalones. Bundling standalones can increase loyal readership or drive sales of a new release. Strategically package standalone, including similar themes by subgenre, location, point in time, similar protagonists, holiday setting, or something else.

315. Include exclusive content in a box set. Adding a novella or short story to a box set could incentivize readers to purchase (instead of buying the books separately). Existing readers might also purchase the box set for the bonus content they haven't seen before.

316. Discount a box set. Running a limited-time sale on box sets can dramatically increase sales, revenue, and visibility. Also, Featured Deals for box sets consistently generate high engagement and conversions from BookBub readers, even when featured at prices higher than $0.99. On average,

we've seen 20% higher click-through rates and 29% higher purchase rates on box sets than single books!

317. Publish a multi-author anthology. Partner with other authors to create an anthology of novellas or short stories. If you promote the collection to your audiences, you can each increase your exposure by reaching the other authors' audiences.

318. Participate in live events. Hold book signings at bookstores and conferences. Signings can help drive word-of-mouth exposure and reviews. Don't feel obligated to give away your books for free. Many authors sell books at their signings — purchase a checkout tool like Square to process credit card transactions at a cost of 2.75% per swipe.

319. Give a talk at a relevant conference. Flex your public speaking skills. As a published author, you can talk about various topics, including the subject of your book, your writing process, your publication journey, and the experience you've had promoting your books and connecting with readers.

320. Participate on panels you're invited to. If flying solo on stage sounds too intimidating, participating on a panel might be a more comfortable option. Speaking on panels at book conferences is a sure way to gain exposure to fans of the other authors on the forum, whether they're readers at consumer conferences or fellow authors at writing conferences.

321. Print business cards to hand out at events. Always carry around something to hand out to potential readers who want to buy your book later. You can create postcard-sized handouts or business cards people can stick in their wallets with a URL to visit your website and purchase your books.

322. Run a contest to draw people to your event. Build buzz and excitement for your signing, session, or panel by offering a free book or giveaway to the first 5–10 people who arrive at each location. Announce this giveaway on your social profiles using the event-specific hashtag. Once other attendees see people flocking to you, they'll want to see what all the fuss is about.

323. Partner with relevant local organizations. For a middle-grade book, coordinate with local PTAs to organize a school reading during a bake sale or book fair. For a thriller about racecar drivers, run a promotion with the nearest track. For a sci-fi book, sponsor a themed party or host a signing at a sci-fi convention.

324. Concentrate marketing efforts in a single week. Bestseller lists are based on the number of units sold each week. Target one list to optimize for its cycle. Focus your campaigns, including price promotions, social media contests, and email marketing, within one week to boost your chances of hitting the list.

325. Pitch a book as a holiday gift. Depending on the type of book you're promoting, the giftable nature of a physical book may help boost print book sales, especially around the holidays. Consider timing your price promotions and ad campaigns around holiday or special, relevant events to increase sales and visibility.

326. Donate books to relevant organizations. If you're promoting a middle-grade book, consider donating a few copies to a summer camp, children's hospital, or school library. Donate to retirement homes, hospitals, and community centers if you're promoting books that appeal to an older

demographic. This can help spark future word-of-mouth sales.

327. Regularly refresh your metadata. Choose 3-5 keywords that best reflect the content of a book based on current trends and how readers are now searching for that content. Swap these keywords into your metadata (such as in the keyword fields and description).

## You Are Ready to Market Your Books

We have covered a lot of ground in this chapter on marketing strategies. Certainly, I have repeated certain themes in this extensive list. To be as comprehensive as possible, I used a lot of different resources, and the overlap was extensive across these references. It is better to repeat important themes than to overlook any.

I have done my best in a limited amount of time to prepare for this next phase of my own book writing and publishing life. I couldn't wait any longer to get to the most serious level of marketing engagement of my publishing career.

I NEED to get to 1,000 book sales per month. The coming season will be quite daunting as I have placed a lot on the table. It may be out of my reach, or anyone else's for that matter, to get to all of the strategies and tactics that have been noted. Still, getting started is key. Finding which recommended actions produce the greatest return on investment will be key. A lot of testing, probing, analytics, and resetting will be required before I get it tweaked optimally.

It will be a beautiful journey as I make these needed changes to my career as a professional author. I hope to look back at this moment of completion of The Art of the Book Hustle and see that this was the smartest move possible. I wish you the best in placing your books in the marketplace.

# Bibliography & Resources

110 Book Marketing Ideas to Sell Your Book In 2023 [https://www.smithpublicity.com/110-book-marketing-ideas-to-sell-your-book/]

119 Book Marketing Ideas to Help Authors Increase Sales, by Diana Urban, Mar 2020 [https://insights.bookbub.com/book-marketing-ideas/]

70+ Book Marketing Ideas to Rocket-Boost Your Sales [https://blog.reedsy.com/book-marketing-ideas/]

The Elements of Style: With Revisions, an Introduction and a Chapter on Writing – William Strunk Jr., E.B. White (2000)

From Pen to Power: Write and Publish Your Book in 90 Days – Keidi Awadu (2023)

Let's Get Digital: How To Self-Publish, And Why You Should – David Gaughran (2011)

Your First 1000 Copies: The Step-by-Step Guide to Marketing Your Book – Tim Grahl (2013)

APE: Author, Publisher, Entrepreneur - How to Publish a Book – Guy Kawasaki and Shawn Welch (2013)

Write. Publish. Repeat.: The No-Luck Guide to Self-Publishing Success – Johnny B. Truant and Sean Platt (2013)

Book Launch: How to Write, Market & Publish Your First Bestseller in Three Months or Less AND Use it to Start and Grow a Six-Figure Business – Chandler Bolt and James Roper (2015)

Sell More Books With Less Social Media: Spend less time marketing and more time writing – Chris Syme (2015)

Mastering Amazon Ads: An Author's Guide – " by Brian Meeks (2018)

# Index

48-Hour Books, 44
ad copy, 42, 88
advertisement, 34, 36, 71
affiliate programs, 63
Alder, Shannon L., 5, 6
Amazon, 21, 22, 45, 47, 48, 51, 52, 54, 55, 58, 62, 63, 69, 70, 80, 84, 98
analytics, 43, 63, 66
anger, 50
Apple, 34
author bio, 60, 64
authors, 1
autobiography, 64
avatar, 61
back matter, 54, 80, 83, 84, 86, 93
Barnes & Noble, 62
blogging, 65
blogs, 23, 33, 65, 77, 84, 88, 89
book funnel, 42
book launch, 22, 53, 63, 71, 72, 87
book trailer, 21, 63, 73, 74
BookBub, 22, 39, 51, 54, 66, 77, 78, 79, 81, 82, 83, 86, 87, 93
brand allure, 37
brand loyalty, 33, 34, 35, 36, 38
Chesson, Dave, 24, 51, 53
click-through rate

CTR, 48
consumer behavior, 33, 35
consumers, 34, 36
contests, 64, 73, 84, 91, 93, 95
copyright, 1
cross-promote, 61, 93
culture, 1, 3, 5
customer loyalty, 34
demographic, 56
eBook, 47, 66
education professionals, 61
electronic media kit, 60
email, 1, 21, 33, 46, 47, 51, 54, 55, 58, 60, 63, 65, 77, 78, 79, 82, 83, 84, 85, 87, 88, 95
emotional appeal, 33, 35
emotional words, 49
emotions, 33, 34, 35, 42
evidence, 18, 35
exclusivity, 37
Facebook, 20, 21, 22, 54, 58, 59, 67, 69, 73, 78, 82, 84, 85, 89, 90, 91, 92, 93
Fair Use, 1
fear, 50
fear of missing out
FOMO, 37
forums, 33, 59, 66
Goodreads, 21, 22, 62, 70, 71, 84
GoodReads, 48

greed, 50
hashtags, 67
Hemingway, Ernest, 2
history, 1
human psychology, 38
impulsive purchasing, 37
innovation, 34
interactive community, 60
keywords, 21, 48, 49, 55, 56, 57, 61, 68, 69, 77, 81, 88, 96
Kindle Direct Publishing, 44, 46
Kindle eBook, 47
Kindlepreneur, 44, 46, 47, 49, 51, 53, 55
landing page, 42, 43
lead magnet, 61
libraries, 61, 95
logic, 3, 33, 35, 36, 42
logical reasoning, 35, 36
marketing and sales, 60
marketing strategies, 58
marketplace, 11, 33, 35, 45, 46, 53, 60, 72
memory retention, 34
merch, 60
merchandise, 42, 61, 64, 71, 86
metadata, 21, 96
mystery, 50
narrative, 4
neuroscientific research, 34
newsletter, 23
newsletters, 33, 39, 65

niche categories, 61
Nike, 16, 34
nonfiction, 8, 49, 55, 56, 67, 74, 76, 92
non-fiction, 1
online payments, 60
pay-per-click advertising, 65
perceptions, 34, 35
persuasion, 35, 36
pre-orders, 63
press release, 63, 89
prestige, 37
print-on-demand
   POD, 44, 45, 46
publisher, 1
publishing, 1
radio, 22, 47, 63, 72, 76
Reddit, 92
romance, 49, 93
RSS Feed, 65
scarcity, 33, 37, 38, 42
science, 1
smartphones, 68
social media, 2, 20, 21, 22, 33, 38, 39, 51, 53, 54, 58, 62, 64, 66, 67, 71, 73, 77, 78, 79, 83, 88, 90, 95
speaking tour, 63
special interest blogs, 65
stimuli, 34
street team, 63, 92
subconscious, 34
superfans, 61
sustainable development, 1
swag, 60, 84

technology, 16, 35
television, 63
trust, 50
Twitter, 16, 20, 52, 67, 68, 69, 73, 78, 85, 89, 90, 91
upselling, 42
urgency, 37, 38
virtual book tour, 65

virtual platforms, 64
vocal style, 62
website SEO, 65
websites, 33, 39, 48, 74, 84, 89
YouTube, 54, 59, 68, 69, 79, 88, 92

# SOME OF THE MOST POPULAR BOOKS BY KEIDI AWADU

100+ Lifespan

Big Up Manhood

Paradigm Shift

Transforming Soul Food

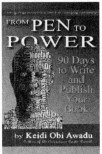
Fade to Black

The Repairing

Global Wellness Future

A.I. Has a God Complex

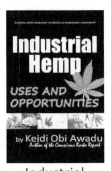
Industrial Hemp

Miracle on Two Feet

Mind Control

The Blackest Soil

See these and many more books and DVDs at

# www.Keidi.biz/CRP2012

Learn about our popular classes at www.CoachKeidi.com

Printed in Great Britain
by Amazon

27583376R00059